Upside Your Head!

MUSIC/CULTURE

A series from Wesleyan University Press

Edited by George Lipsitz, Susan McClary, and Robert Walser

JOHNNY OTIS

Upside Your Head!

RHYTHM AND BLUES

ON

CENTRAL AVENUE

Introduction by
GEORGE LIPSITZ

WESLEYAN UNIVERSITY PRESS

Published by University Press of New England

Hanover & London

WESLEYAN UNIVERSITY PRESS
Published by University Press of New England, Hanover, NH 03755
© 1993 by Johnny Otis
All rights reserved
Printed in the United States of America 5 4 3 2 1
CIP data appear at the end of the book

I dedicate this book to my following loved ones:

My wife: Phyllis
My sons: Shuggie, Nicky, Buddy, Robert, and Darryl Jon
My daughters: Janice, Laura, and Stephanie
My grandsons: Chris, Mike, Lucky, Kevin, Gamal, Little Buddy,
Eric, Niki, Andre, Bobby, Jr., Iian, John, Craig, Aaron
My granddaughters: Nicole, Cameo, Saran, Louvenia
My great granddaughters: Jhlequa, Trimesia

With a special thanks to my lifetime friends:
William "Blick" Avant, Preston Love, and Hal Kronick

Contents

Illustrations

Preface

I was half-finished writing this book when the Rodney King events exploded. All of a sudden, *Rhythm and Blues* as a title was out, and *Upside Your Head!* was in. I was having trouble staying strictly with music anyhow, and now I decided not to limit this book to music only.

In 1965, I wrote a book titled *Listen to the Lambs*. Someone at W.W. Norton Publishing Company read a letter I had written to author Griff Borgeson about my experiences in Watts during the uprising and decided I should write a book. During a golf game in New York, my contact person at W.W. Norton mentioned the project to Columbia Records' John Hammond who pointed out that I was a musician. It was then suggested that I include my musical experiences.

This time around, just the opposite has happened. Wesleyan University Press commissioned me to do a book about rhythm and blues music and the Central Avenue culture in early Los Angeles, but the powerful and tragic events of May 1992 have led me to deal with more than mere music.

The title of my first book, *Listen to the Lambs*, was taken from an old African American spiritual that says the lambs are crying for the Lord to come by and ease their suffering. Well, thirty years have gone by, and the suffering is even more acute and neither the Lord nor anyone else has come by to offer any relief.

What happened to Rodney King comes as no great surprise to the average Black person. The police have been going upside African Americans' heads for centuries. The only change today is that thousands of young Black people have had enough of that shit and are willing to risk the consequences of going upside white heads.

I have never thought that extreme hate groups such as the Ku Klux Klan, Nazis, and so on posed the biggest danger to African Ameri-

The Johnny Otis Band in a recent photograph. From left to right, top row: Paige Smith, Nick Otis, Charles Patterson, Larry Douglas, Tricky Lofton. Middle row: James Clark, Shuggie Otis, Fred Clark, Clifford Solomon, Ronald Wilson. Front row: Jackie Payne, J.O., LaDee Streeter.

cans and other minorities. The real culprits are the average, run-of-the-mill, law-abiding white Americans. Those who go to church, mow their lawns, and deplore racism and injustice. When something as horrendous as the Rodney King beating is thrust in their faces, they are outraged but actually do nothing more than cluck their tongues. They are terribly uneasy at times like these because deep down in their subconscious, buried under a mountain of disclaimers and justifications, they know goddamned well that they are to blame.

Just as in the aftermath of the Watts riots, it is once again the time of the commissions and of the blue-ribbon panels. The words "race relations," "healing," and "renewal" are bandied about. It is time, once again, to "study" the racial situation.

A racist president arrives in Los Angeles after the rioting and insults us by declaring he has come to learn. Just imagine . . . the Willie Horton president . . . the elected leader of the most advanced country in the world claims he is ignorant about racial injustice and has to learn about the most malignant social cancer in our society. If that isn't insulting, it is surely pathetic.

The old saying goes, we get exactly what we deserve when we elect people to office, but I wouldn't wish a Reagan or a Bush on a dog. What we deserve in America is a powerful visionary. Some strong and principled woman or man who will lead us out of the quagmire of racism and economic inequity. We need a president who can show the American people that corporate fascism and racial injustice will destroy the nation, and we need to advance programs to eliminate both.

Mort Sahl once said, "We know that communism doesn't work, but what about capitalism?" What we have in America is predatory capitalism. We are told we live under a free enterprise system but, not so. We may feel good about calling it free enterprise but Conspiracy of the Rich and Greedy is a more accurate description. The average white American is a victim of predatory capitalism's conspiracy too, but people of color have an extra demon to cope with in racism.

The racists in the U.S. government send billions in aid to Europe and Israel but say "to hell" with the American citizens languishing in the inner-city ghettos. Common sense should tell us to take care of our own first, but instead we are preoccupied with funneling our tax dollars to white countries overseas. In the process, the United States is building "good will" (it thinks) in Poland, Rumania, Israel, Russia, and the like. But time will tell how much "goodwill" U.S. dollars will buy in Eastern Europe and Israel.

There is no doubt about how much "ill will" continued neglect is building in the hearts of Black Americans. In 1965, I wrote that if racism and economic injustice continued to be the lot of African Americans ("Negroes" was the politically correct term at that time), then Watts was just a rehearsal for terrible things to come. Now that a crushing terrible thing *has* come, I wonder if the U.S. government and whites in general see the handwriting on the wall? Probably not. America has always used the threat of going upside your head as the answer to unrest. Well, I suspect that ain't gonna work too good any more. After a few more blue-ribbon committee studies and bullshit platitudes from elected officials and the press and some assuaging round table TV discussions, the status quo will once again prevail. All the activity after the Watts and

Los Angeles riots focuses on the effects of a sick society. Nary a word about the real causes behind the sickness. But all this motion will create the effect of action, and things will probably calm down again for a while. Given the crucial catalyst, every big American city with a sizable African American population could go up in flames all at once. Then who will be going upside whose head?

Creating Dangerously:
The Blues Life of Johnny Otis

George Lipsitz

In *Upside Your Head!*, Johnny Otis presents the kinds of information and insight that only he can provide: details about the hidden links between rhythm & blues and jazz, disclosure of the secret language of Lester Young and the secret heartaches of Esther Phillips, and discussions about the elements unifying Black communities all across the nation. But most importantly, Johnny Otis testifies to the endurance and imagination of African American culture.

A popular old joke among African Americans illustrates the importance of understanding the context in which Black cultural creativity takes place. In the joke, a white Southern plantation owner wants to rebut criticism that Blacks are oppressed in his state. He orders one of his Black sharecroppers to accompany him to a radio station, so he can make a broadcast affirming how well he has been treated by whites. The sharecropper hesitates at first, expressing qualms about public speaking and voicing worries that he might make a mistake. But the plantation owner prevails by explaining that people from coast to coast are waiting to hear what the sharecropper has to say. After getting reassurance that the broadcast will indeed reach the whole nation, the sharecropper steps up to the microphone, cups his hands around his mouth, and hollers "H-E-E-E-ELP!"[1]

In some ways, Black music in the United States has been like that broadcast. Denied access to many other avenues of expression, African American musicians have used the power and appeal of their art to fashion powerful critiques of the realities that Black people face every day—

From left, Jimmy Nolen, Johnny Otis, Freddy Harmon, Robbie Robinson, George Washington, and Don Johnson. Trumpeter Don Johnson scored a Top Twenty rhythm and blues hit in 1949 with "Jackson's Blues." Guitarist Jimmy Nolen went on to become an important part of James Brown's bands.

racial discrimination, economic exploitation, and cultural suppression. But Black music is much more than a simple response to white racism; it is a complicated and complex expression of the totality of African American culture—its joy, triumph, imagination, desire, wisdom, and moral strength. It has been what the philosopher Albert Camus called "a dangerous creation," a disclosure of feelings and philosophies that powerful forces try to keep hidden. Creating art under those circumstances according to Camus, "exposes one to the passions of an age that forgives nothing."[2]

Many people have been captured by the beauty and power of Black music: Johnny Otis is one of them. Born in 1921, Otis grew up in a Greek immigrant family that ran a grocery store in an ethnically mixed but mostly Black neighborhood in Berkeley, California. He remembers that his first fascination with Black culture came from accompanying some of his Black playmates to church. The churches provided Graham crackers and chocolate milk for children, and in those times Graham crackers and chocolate milk were rare delicacies to him. But Otis soon realized that it was more than the Graham crackers and the chocolate milk; that the sounds of the gospel choirs, the enthusiasm of the congregations, and the intellectual and moral power of the preachers spoke to him in profound ways. "That culture captured me," he remembers, explaining that it seemed more immediate and relevant and open to him than his own culture—the Greek American culture that came to him through his parents' phonograph records or through the Greek language lessons he struggled through in the basement of Greek churches on afternoons when he would rather have been out playing.[3]

When a high school teacher criticized him for spending too much time with Blacks and not associating enough with whites, Otis culminated his long running battle with educational authorities by dropping out of school. He took up the life of a professional musician as a member of Count Otis Matthews's West Oakland House Rockers. He married his high school sweetheart, Phyllis Walker, and served an apprenticeship with "territory" jazz bands in the Midwest before moving to Los Angeles in 1943. He changed his name from John Veliotes to Johnny Otis and began to think of himself as "Black by persuasion." For more than fifty years, he has served the Los Angeles African American community in many capacities—not only as a music performer, producer, promoter, and night club owner but also as an artist, a radio and television personality, a civil rights activist, and as the pastor of a nondenominational sanctified church.

For Otis, identity has been more a matter of culture than of color; living as a "Black" man has enabled Johnny Otis to be a part of the world that he understands best and that means the most to him. Of course, he has always known that there are some dimensions of the African American experience that he cannot feel; that his biological makeup has always allowed him the theoretical option of living as "white." But his absorption in Black culture has become such an internalized part of his experience that he finds it impossible to think of himself in any other terms.

Like some of those Euro-Americans "captured" by Native American tribes in early U.S. history, Otis became an extremely ferocious defender of his adopted community and an equally zealous opponent of white supremacy. As a civil rights activist, he joined picket lines pro-

Charles Brown and Johnny Otis in Los Angeles, 1969.

testing against segregation and worked tirelessly to raise money for the struggle. As an entertainer, he has used his visibility and his skills to call attention on his radio and television broadcasts to the poisonous effects of white racism. As an author, he wrote one of the definitive interpretations of the 1965 Watts riots, a 1968 book titled *Listen to the Lambs*.[4]

Most important, Johnny Otis has lived a life that rebukes racism and its narrow enclosures by creating an intercultural environment in all of his endeavors—one that honors African American traditions and calls upon others to recognize and embrace them. While always acknowledging the centrality of the African American experience to his art, intellect, and morality, Otis has assembled music groups that have included people from diverse backgrounds—African American, Euro-American, Mexican American, Afro-Asian, and many others. His predominately Black congregation at the Landmark Community Church included whites, Latinos, and Asians in a Christian congregation that even had a few members who were Jewish and a few who were Buddhist. Unabashedly pro-Black and anti-white supremacist, Otis has carried on his part of the struggle by creating panethnic antiracist communities in music, religion, politics, and business.

Johnny Otis is best known for his many successes as a musician, songwriter, and band leader, but he has racked up many other achievements in the course of his fascinating life. His paintings and works of sculpture have been widely exhibited and celebrated. He has been an unsuccessful candidate for elective office and a successful organic farmer and apple juice manufacturer.

As a musician, Johnny Otis wrote and recorded "Willie and the Hand Jive," one of the most popular rock and roll songs of all time. He also wrote the beautiful "Every Beat of My Heart," which later became a hit for Gladys Knight and the Pips. He played the drums on Big Mama Thornton's recording of "Hound Dog," as well as on Illinois Jacquet's "Flying Home," and Charles Brown's "Drifting Blues." He played the haunting introduction on vibraphone to Johnny Ace's "Pledging My

Johnny Otis at his twenty-first birthday party.

Love." He discovered, recorded, and promoted great stars including Big Mama Thornton, Little Willie John, Little Esther Phillips, and the Three Tons of Joy. (And probably some normal-size people too!) Otis has made a specialty out of discovering and nurturing the talents of female vocalists through his professional associations with Ernestine Anderson, Esther Phillips, Etta James, Margie Evans, Linda Hopkins, Sugar Pie Di Santo, and Marie Adams. He has also discovered other stars; one day in Detroit in the early 1950s, Otis conducted a talent contest and discovered Little Willie John, Hank Ballard, and Jackie Wilson—all in one afternoon!

Otis's experiences have brought him in direct contact with some of the most important figures in African American life and culture. As a musician, he has worked with Charlie Parker, Lester Young, Art Tatum, and Count Basie. He became acquainted with the great poet Langston Hughes and the future Supreme Court Justice Thurgood Marshall in night clubs when they came up to the bandstand and introduced themselves as enthusiastic fans of his music. He became a friend of Maya Angelou in the 1950s. Otis has participated in discussions about racism and the struggle to combat it with people from every stratum of life, including James Baldwin and Malcolm X. The television star and comedian Redd Foxx worked as Otis's assistant during his days as a radio disc jockey, and the actress Lawanda ("Aunt Esther") Page was a member of Otis's congregation at the Landmark Community Church.

When he started out with Count Otis Matthews and the West Oakland House Rockers, Johnny Otis grew impatient with the small ensemble sound of the House Rockers and with playing gymnasium dances for only a big jug of red wine to be divided among all the musicians. He aspired to be a big band musician, to play in the aggregations that he so admired like those fronted by Count Basie, Jimmy Lunceford, or Duke Ellington. But years later, when Otis understood more fully the importance of the blues tradition, he realized that he had acquired a rich musical education while playing with the West Oakland House Rockers. "Sometimes you just don't know where it's at," he recalled later. "But it was good as experience and a valuable lesson, because as I moved on I began to realize that true artistic expression and talent is taken lightly and for granted—very often even dismissed or ridiculed. When Little Esther, Mel Walker, Pete Lewis, Big Mama Thornton, Delmar Evans, Shuggie [Otis], Margie Evans, Etta James, Sugarcane Harris, et cetera, came along, I knew exactly what I was dealing with, even if they didn't realize their own magical gifts, or the world ignored them. Fortunately, sooner or later, they were recognized."[5]

NEGRO ACHIEVEMENTS

A MAGAZINE FOR EVERYBODY

eaturing Negro A̶c̶h̶i̶e̶v̶e̶m̶e̶n̶ts And True Stories

Exclusive;
CCESSFUL PASTORATE
REVEREND L. L. WILLIAMS

JOHNNY OTIS

READ ABOUT:
$100.00
PRIZE STORY
CONTEST

25¢   OCTOBER 1951

Cover of *Negro Achievements* magazine, October 1951.

When Otis first went to Los Angeles, he played drums for Harlan
Leonard's Kansas City Rockets. He stayed on in the city to play in
Bardu Ali's band, and by 1945 he had formed a sixteen-piece group that
served as the house band at the Club Alabam. Otis began playing drums
on recording dates, accompanying Illinois Jacquet, Lester Young, and
Charles Brown. His first hit record came in 1946 with "Harlem Noc-

Dallas, Texas, 1952. From left, Fred Ford, Don Johnson, Lady Dee Williams, Johnny Otis, Pete Lewis, and Albert Winston.

turne," featuring Rene Bloch on saxophone. In 1948 he joined with Bardu Ali, his wife Tila Ali, and musician Johnny Miller to open the Barrelhouse Club in Watts—probably the first night spot in the world to feature rhythm and blues music exclusively. From featured acts at the Barrelhouse, Otis assembled the Johnny Otis Rhythm and Blues Caravan that later became the Johnny Otis Show. Propelled by the popularity of Little Esther Phillips, Mel Walker, Red Lyte, and Devonia "Lady Dee" Williams, the Johnny Otis Show had fifteen Top 40 rhythm and blues hits between 1950 and 1952.[6]

Otis's success with live performances and shows led to the opportunity to become a disc jockey on Los Angeles radio and television stations. According to local legend, his radio program was so popular that one could drive along the beach from Los Angeles down to San Diego with no radio in your car, but still hear the Johnny Otis Show blaring out from portable radios and car radios all along the beach. In 1955 he started the Dig Records label in a studio in his garage but later moved into an office building where he could broadcast his radio program, rehearse the television show, and still supervise the production of phonograph records. At the same time, he continued to record hit records himself and to serve as a talent scout for other labels such as Don Robey's Peacock Records from Houston.

The early postwar period was an exhilarating time for Johnny Otis, and not just because of his successful career. The era seemed to mark a turning point for race relations in the United States as well. For many African Americans, Charlie Parker's 1945 song "Now's the Time" an-

Preston Love (with Dennis Lyles) shortly after leaving the Johnny Otis Band and starting his own group in 1953. Love played with Otis in the territory bands and in Otis's Los Angeles groups, wrote the preface to Otis's book *Listen To The Lambs*, and has been one of Johnny's closest friends. As a musician, Love joins Earl Warren and Willie Smith among great lead alto sax players in the history of jazz.

nounced the dawn of a new era. Militant civil rights activity among returning war veterans and the Black anti-draft movement organized by A. Philip Randolph seemed to complement the extraordinarily intense cultural creativity manifested in the emergence of writers, including Ralph Ellison, Chester Himes, and Ann Petry. "I saw the whole community lifting," Otis recalls. "I thought we were going to realize the American Dream. . . . [We would say] it's a bitch, there's still a lot of racism, but it's going to be OK because our kids will realize a fresh new democratic America. Oh, how wrong we were."[7]

As Black unemployment began to reach levels three times that of whites, and as urban renewal demolished the infrastructure of African American communities all across the country, municipal officials joined with moralists (and the major recording companies with their rosters of mostly white artists) to attack rhythm and blues—to censor its sales and radio exposure, to close down night clubs and dance halls where races mingled, and to prosecute entertainers and promoters on "morals" charges rarely faced by artists in other branches of popular music. As Otis remembers, in those years, "Things were grim, and I realized that my original appraisal had been accurate and my new enthusiasm and happiness were not well-founded, unfortunately: that the majority did not give a shit about Black folk, and in fact despised them. That's been the big question in my life. I've got to figure that one out. Instead of thanking God for the African presence, 'cause they've been a great gift to this country . . . and they constantly attempted to share this gift, and always [were] rebuffed and always used and abused, not accepted."[8]

Driven out of the city of Los Angeles by police harassment against youths attending rock and roll shows, Johnny Otis and other music entrepreneurs moved their shows to El Monte Legion Stadium in Los Angeles County. These shows, which often drew 2,000 people a night, have been immortalized in songs by Frank Zappa, Captain Beefheart, the Penguins, and Ruben Guevara as a golden age in local rock and roll history. The proximity of El Monte to large concentrations of Mexican Americans augmented the intercultural dialogue that had always been a part of this music. The Black saxophonist Chuck Higgins became a big favorite among Mexican American young people, and he recorded his hit record "Pachuko Hop" in tribute to their distinctive dress and dance styles. Johnny Otis had long enjoyed a substantial Mexican American following, largely because of shows he performed at Angelus Hall in East L.A., and during his years at El Monte he discovered, produced, and promoted the first Chicano R&B sensation, L'il Julian Herrera, who scored an enormous local hit with his Black-style ballad "Lonely Lonely

Nights" in 1956. One day a probation officer showed up at Otis's door asking about a "Ron Gregory." Otis didn't know anyone by that name, but when the officer showed him a picture, he recognized L'il Julian. It seems that Herrera was a Hungarian Jew from the East Coast named Ron Gregory, who had run away from home and been taken in by a woman in Boyle Heights who raised him as her son. Thus, the first L.A. Chicano rock and roll star turned out to be a Hungarian Jew, produced and promoted by a Greek who thought of himself as Black!

In 1956, the El Monte City Council revoked the dance permit they has issued to Johnny Otis's partner, Hal Zeiger, on the grounds that "rock and roll creates an unwholesome, unhealthy situation." But disc jockeys Al Jarvis and Hunter Hancock, as well as representatives of the American Civil Liberties Union, the National Association for the Advancement of Colored People, and American Federation of Musicians Local 47, joined Johnny Otis in protesting the decision as an instance of racism, as a measure designed primarily to prevent young people from mingling in a mixed-race situation. They succeeded in having the ban rescinded, but rock and roll still encountered systematic opposition from powerful forces.[9]

By the late 1950s, federal, state, and local government pressure, combined with private censorship, effectively destroyed the radio stations, record labels, and urban dance halls that had nurtured rhythm and blues. The largest corporations in the music industry regained control of the market with a watered down and whitened up music which they sold as "rock and roll." Johnny Otis wound up on Capitol records where he had one of his biggest hits, "Willie and the Hand Jive," in 1958. But his experience with that company was not a good one. "My Capitol Records time was very lucrative in dollars and cents, but very negative creatively," he remembers. "I tried to chase the almighty dollar and listened to bad advice from profit-motivated sources when I should have been my own Black self, recording my own Black R&B sounds, and not have gone into contrived rock and roll shit. With a few exceptions of which 'Willie and the Hand Jive' is one, I am quite unhappy with some of the directions I took in those days."[10]

Johnny Otis started producing records for the King label in 1961, but the music business became increasingly resistant to rhythm and blues. The popularity of the Beatles increased the size of the industry tremendously, as young rock and rollers received lucrative contracts and enormous promotion budgets. Yet the Black artists whose innovations made rock and roll possible in the first place continued to face a contracting market. The dimensions of these changes came home to Otis one night

The Johnny Otis Show, El Monte Legion Stadium. When municipal harassment forced rock and roll dances outside the city limits, Johnny Otis and other entrepreneurs took their music to El Monte Legion Stadium. Because El Monte was conveniently located near East Los Angeles and other Chicano neighborhoods, the concerts there enhanced intercultural communication, mixing Mexican Americans, African Americans, Asian Americans, and Euro-Americans together in shared enthusiasm for Black music.

in the sixties when he reported for a night club job and found that they had no piano. "What piano?" the club owner asked incredulously. "I thought you were a guitar player! Nobody plays piano anymore."[11]

The increased segregation of the music industry mirrored a similar trend in society at large, leading Johnny Otis to join millions of others in civil rights activism. He sought the Democratic Party's nomination for a seat in the California State Assembly twice in the 1960s and served as chief of staff in the Los Angeles office of Mervyn Dymally, who held office as a member of the California legislature, as the state's lieutenant governor, and as a member of Congress in the seventies and eighties. In Johnny Otis's book about the 1968 Watts Riots, he drew on his own experiences as a resident of Los Angeles to observe, "The races have grown so isolated from one another in big urban areas like Los Angeles, that it is sheer nonsense to ask the majority what's plaguing the minority. Even if there were any demonstrable evidence upon which to base the belief that whites, in general, harbor concern for Negroes' welfare, it would be impossible for them to have any inkling of what might be bugging the Black man across town with whom he never has social contact and rarely even sees."[12]

Johnny's son Shuggie had started playing guitar professionally at the age of twelve and soon found himself employed playing lead guitar, bass, and keyboards on recording sessions for a variety of artists. In 1968, Johnny Otis recorded and produced an album for Kent Records, *Cold Shot*, that featured fifteen-year-old Shuggie on lead guitar along with appearances by several veterans of the Los Angeles rhythm and blues scene, including Don "Sugarcane" Harris and Delmar Evans. They had no guarantee that the album would even be released, but it became a big seller, generated a hit single on the rhythm and blues charts, led to a producer's contract with Columbia-Epic records for Johnny Otis, and helped to secure artist's contracts for Shuggie, Johnny, Delmar Evans, and Don Harris. The sizzling guitar solos of Shuggie Otis introduced a whole new generation of fans to the Johnny Otis Show and consequently to the rhythm and blues traditions that too easily became forgotten in the enthusiasm for rock and roll in the sixties.

In the seventies, Otis recorded and produced albums by legendary artists, including Louis Jordan, Joe Liggins, and T-Bone Walker. Recording these on small, independent labels meant sacrificing the wide distribution networks available to the major companies, but it also allowed him an element of artistic control that would not have been possible otherwise. At the same time he began broadcasting his weekly three-hour radio program on listener-sponsored FM radio stations in the Los Angeles area. Otis's experiences as a promoter, producer, and bandleader have always required him to understand and master the demands of the business, but he has often been critical of the practices of commerce and capitalism that he has encountered.

Predatory capitalism is based on profit and power, it has no consideration for artistry or cultural integrity. . . . When we go to Europe where there are [also] capitalist economies, it's not the same. They pay some attention to cultural questions. But here, . . . you wind up with these power and profit mongers now having at their disposal the electronic means to grab people from almost the cradle and to cater to the most juvenile tastes. They're able to condition these young people before these youngsters have had enough experiences and enough input of a varied type to make a decent artistic decision. So they make up their minds for them, the major product manufacturers sponsor them, so that by the time the kid's ten or twelve, he's a lost cause in terms of artistic appreciation.[13]

Alienation from the music industry's corruption and concern about the moral problems of society in general, helped to propel Johnny Otis into the ministry. Mother Bernice Smith, a Los Angeles evangelist suggested to Otis that he would make a good preacher. "You mean become Reverend Hand Jive?" he asked with a laugh. But the evangelist recognized the makings of a member of the clergy in his seriousness about social issues, his love for the community, and his capacity to bring people together. She ordained him as a minister, and in the mid-seventies Otis organized the Landmark Community Church. He stressed the importance of people loving one another, and he brought into being a congregation committed to Christian fellowship and social change. Under his leadership, the Church took a prominent public role in combatting hunger in Los Angeles: distributing free food and campaigning for institutional responses to poverty by private charities and by the government. But when Otis saw that the church's social functions always outdrew its efforts to feed the hungry, he concluded that he had not really gotten his message across, and he disbanded the church in the mid-eighties.[14]

In the nineties, Johnny Otis continues to play music all over the world, to discover new talent, and to produce and promote the jazz and blues that have meant so much to him throughout his life. His paintings and pieces of sculpture appear regularly in art exhibits and galleries, and he devotes much of his time these days to organic farming and to the production and distribution of his organic Johnny Otis Apple Juice. But all of his extraordinary individual endeavors and achievements have not dimmed his passion for racial justice. On his weekly radio broadcasts on Pacifica listener-sponsored radio stations in Berkeley, Fresno, and Los Angeles, and in his other public appearances, Johnny Otis continues his crusade against white supremacy. He also continues to create spaces for panethnic antiracism, for diverse communities capable of honoring African American traditions and uniting around their humane sensibilities. Perhaps none of his activities typifies this spirit as much as the annual Johnny Otis Red Beans and Rice Family Festival.

The 1992 festival took on special significance in the wake of the Los Angeles rebellion of that year. Less than four months after popular anger against the verdict in the Rodney King trial (and against almost twenty years of deprivation and resurgent racism) exploded in one of the bloodiest and most destructive civil disorders in U.S. history, thousands of Angelenos from different backgrounds gathered in a Los Angeles County park in San Dimas for Johnny Otis's annual festival.

Few events could have attracted such a diverse crowd. Latino food vendors from East Los Angeles served *helados* from Whittier Boulevard *paleterias*, while next to them African American cooks offered red beans and rice. Crowds lined up for Jamaican jerk chicken, Chinese egg rolls, and Italian pizza. A group of elderly African American men played dominoes under the trees in one section of the grounds, while Chicano car customizers showed off a beautiful aqua 1951 Mercury and two splendid mid-fifties Chevrolets in another grove. Mixed-race

With Lady Dee Williams, Apollo Theatre, New York, 1950.

couples and families strolled the grounds, chatted pleasantly, and shared food with what seemed like every imaginable combination of people. All week long, our televisions had been broadcasting the Republican National Convention where speaker after speaker insisted that there could only be one kind of family, one kind of sexuality, one kind of patriotism, and one kind of culture. But here under the hot sun just four months after a deadly riot, people were demonstrating that there are many different ways to live and that difference can be a source of strength as well as a cause of conflict.

For almost ten hours, nearly a dozen musical aggregations performed music steeped in the rhythm and blues traditions of Los Angeles. Young Chicano bodybuilders with long loose *cholo* shorts and no shirts showed off their elaborate tattoos while dancing with their Anglo dates. A group of Black women wearing heavy metal T-shirts cheered the tribute to African American rhythm and blues singer Little Richard presented by Chicano singer Ernie Valenzuela, the cousin of Ritchie Valens, one of

Johnny Otis and Bo Diddley. Born Ellas McDaniel in 1928, Bo Diddley moved from Mississippi to Chicago in 1934 and became an important part of rhythm and blues and blues music in that city. He recorded eleven Top Forty rhythm and blues hits between 1955 and 1967.

the great Mexican-American rock and roll heroes. Middle-aged white and Black couples got up to slow-dance to Chicana Rosie Hamlin singing her great hit "Angel Baby," while the Chicano band Thee Midnighters serenaded Chicanas in shorts and halter tops mouthing the words of the ballad "That's All" as they danced cheek to cheek with their Black dance partners. The Black band War came out in tie-dyed T-shirts with peace signs on them, and they created a commotion among Mexican Americans enthusiastic about their Afro-Cuban sounds. A white man and his Asian American female partner danced the jitterbug to the Penguins rendition of the Latino flavored rhythm and blues favorite, "Hey Senorita."

The voices from the bandstand made frequent references to the riots. African American singer Richard Berry did "There's a Riot Goin' On," adding a verse about April 1992. Ernie Valenzuela sang "Framed," (a fifties song written by two Jews for a Black vocal group but also recorded by Ernie's Chicano cousin Ritchie Valens) about a man harassed by the police. Lonnie Jordan, keyboard player for War, emphasized a line in his group's "Why Can't We Be Friends" to make a conciliatory gesture to Asian Americans in clear reference to the tensions between African Americans and Korean Americans in Los Angeles in recent months. But the common memory of the terrible divisions exposed by the riots did not obscure the unity in diversity celebrated in the festival.

The common musical memories that knitted that crowd together clearly played an important role in people's life histories. The intercultural content of the music demonstrated how thoroughly diverse ethnic groups have been implicated in one another's lives. At the festival, it became obvious that it would have been very difficult to grow up Anglo or Latino or Black or Native American or Asian American in Los Angeles without being formed in some way by the meeting of cultures that came across so clearly in the music and the subcultural activities associated with it. As the day drew to a close, people rushed toward the stage to be close to the Johnny Otis Show, to end the day in total absorption with the sounds, feelings, and memories that brought them there in the first place.

At the center of it all was Johnny Otis, directing a multiracial band and playing in front of a multiracial crowd. Some people in the crowd knew him from his days as a jazz musician, others recalled the rock and roll dances at El Monte Legion Stadium. Some had been members of the Landmark Community Church, and others had listened to him on the radio for many years. But what held them all together was Black music: its captivating and liberating power, as well as Johnny Otis's testimony on behalf of it. His ability to bring people together on that day depended on his lifelong commitment to a community and its culture, but also on the power of Black music itself, the escapes that it has offered, and the truths that it has told people about themselves and about the country in which they live.

One day in the mid-eighties, Johnny Otis preached the eulogy at Big Mama Thornton's funeral. When the service ended and the mourners left the church, one of them commented on the tears streaming down Johnny Otis's cheeks: "Oh, Johnny, we know that you loved Big Mama so much, and you're sorry that she's gone, but think of the good times and the good days." But he was not really crying about Big Mama's death. He was thinking about how lucky he had been to know her, to be part of the community that she came out of, and to be involved with the people he saw at her funeral. Music had made it possible for him to learn about African American culture and to fight for it. "I'm just glad I'm a part of this," he thought to himself.[15]

Johnny Otis is not the only one who is lucky to be "a part of this." People of all ethnicities and nationalities have been nurtured and sustained by the many strengths of Black culture. But we are now at a crossroads, at an unparalleled moment of danger. The resurgent racism of our time provides us with an acid test, and in the years ahead, it seems clear that we will be tested again and again. Many times and in many ways, we will be asked to be racists. At those moments, Johnny Otis's dangerous creations can provide us with a reliable compass with which to steer our course. In a time when we seemed trapped by the legacy and the regeneration of racism, he can show us the way out.

In "Willie and the Hand Jive," Johnny Otis sings about "a cat named Way Out Willie." The beat poet Bob Kaufman used to contend that sometimes "'way out' people know the way out."[16] He meant that what might seem merely unusual, eccentric, or marginal to some might really be central to the futures we all hope to face. Johnny Otis might seem "way out" to a lot of people, but in his unremitting resistance to racism and in his efforts to form panethnic antiracist communities he also shows us the way out.

Notes

1. Lawrence Levine, *Black Culture and Black Consciousness: Afro-American Folk Thought from Slavery to Freedom* (New York: Oxford University Press, 1977), 318. I am indebted to the always observant and always brilliant Robin D. G. Kelley for calling this passage to my attention.

2. Albert Camus, *Resistance, Rebellion, and Death* (New York: Knopf, 1981), 251.

3. Interview with Johnny Otis, December 14, 1986 Altadena, California.

4. Johnny Otis, *Listen to the Lambs* (New York: Norton, 1968).

5. Johnny Otis, "Johnny Otis in His Own Words," *DISCoveries* (February 1990), 24. I thank Gary Burns for directing my attention to this article. Additions to original text made by Johnny Otis in a letter to me on January 12, 1993.

6. Donald Clarke, ed., *The Penguin Encyclopedia of Popular Music* (London: Penguin, 1989), 881–82. Johnny Otis, "Johnny Otis in His Own Words," *DISCoveries* (February 1990), 25; Joel Whitburn, *Top R&B Singles, 1942–1988* (Menomonee Falls, WI: Record Research, 1988), 316–17.

7. Interview with Johnny Otis, December 14, 1986, Altadena, California.

8. Interview with Johnny Otis, December 14, 1986, Altadena, California.

9. "Bias Blasted in Rock'n'Roll Fight." *California Eagle*, August 9, 1956, 1, 4. I thank Mike Davis for directing my attention to this article. For an account of censorship efforts against rock'n'roll, see George Lipsitz, *Time Passages: Collective Memory and American Popular Culture* (Minneapolis: University of Minnesota Press, 1990), 123–27.

10. "Johnny Otis in His Own Words" *DISCoveries* (February 1990), 26. Correspondence, Johnny Otis to George Lipsitz, January 9, 1993.

11. "Johnny Otis in His Own Words" *DISCoveries* (February 1990), 26.

12. Johnny Otis, *Listen to the Lambs* (New York: Norton, 1968), 91.

13. Interview with Johnny Otis, December 14, 1986, Altadena, California.

14. Telephone conversation with Johnny Otis, December 31, 1992.

15. Interview with Johnny Otis, May 25, 1990, Altadena, California.

16. Quoted by Maria Damon, "Unmeaning Jargon," *South Atlantic Quarterly* (Fall) 1988, 708–709.

Upside Your Head!

Central Avenue

During a recent road trip with my show, a poignant remark by one of the old-timers brought on a mood that can only be described as mourning. As the bus rolled through the Midwest on a clear summer night, the air was full of reminiscence. We older guys were recalling the good old days, and the young singers and musicians of the group were listening. Bull Moose Jackson, Preston Love, Freddy Clark, Clora Bryant, and I each offered a memory or an anecdote. Veteran trombonist John "Streamline" Ewing hadn't said much up to this point, but now, from the dim area in the rear of the bus we heard him say in a melancholy tone, "We had it all to ourselves."

The happy conversation died, and it became very quiet. You could cut the feeling of dismay in the air with a knife. An old wound had been opened among the older musicians. The youngsters sat quietly, not quite understanding what all the anguish was about but sensing that something heavy had snuffed out the jubilant mood. The following day, my son Nicky, who plays drums in the band, remarked, "Damn, Dad, I never felt it so quiet and so sad on the bus. What was that all about?"

It was about several things. To begin with, it was about the pensive mood of oldsters when they reflect upon the loss of their youth. There was also the sense of loss at the passing of a golden age. But the deeper and more pervasive source of the pain was the knowledge that racism was the primary factor in the deterioration of African American culture and, mourn as we may, that we are powerless to undo the damage. The silence and sadness that night was finally about bewilderment. . . . How, with things seeming to be moving in the right direction as they were in the forties and fifties, could we lose it all so completely?

The appropriation of African American music by whites sounded a death knell for traditional rhythm and blues artists in the fifties. Rockabillies and other whites lifted the black blues and boogie creations en masse. The major record companies and radio stations went full blast behind the white imitators, while the original African American art form took a beating. Once again, as had happened in the case of earlier black musical styles—Dixieland, big band swing, and modern jazz, whites reaped a rich reward from concepts they didn't invent.

When Duke Ellington's great balladeer, Herb Jeffries, looks back and says, "Central Avenue was our Harlem Renaissance," he echoes the sentiments of all who lived through that fertile and creative time before, during, and after World War II. The history of rhythm and blues music in Los Angeles is inseparably tied to the development of the African American culture that formed and flourished in the Central Avenue

Johnny Otis and his Orchestra, the Club Alabam, Los Angeles, 1946. Top row from left: Eddie Preston, Lester Current, Billy Jones, Loyal Walker (trumpets), John Pettigrew, George Washington, Herb Mullins (trombones). Front row from left: Bernie Cobb (guitar), Cliff Trenier (vocal), Leon Beck (baritone sax), Kent Pope (alto sax), Johnny Otis (vibes), Paul Quinchette (tenor sax), James Von Streeter (tenor sax), Lee Wesley Jones (piano), Curtis Counce (bass), Claude Trenier (vocal).

Twins Claude and Clifford Trenier sang with the Jimmie Lunceford Band in 1944 and 1945, and recorded for Mercury as the Trenier Twins between 1947 and 1950. With their brothers Buddy and Milt they formed the Treniers and had a hit with "Go Go Go" in 1951. Their wild stage show became the model for many subsequent R&B and rock acts.

9/3/45

Paul Quinchette, Johnny Otis, Phyllis Otis, Frances Harris, and Robert Harris at the Club Alabam, 1945.

Quinchette played tenor saxophone with bands fronted by Jay McShann, Benny Carter, Big Sid Catlett, Louis Jordan, Lucky Millinder, and Count Basie as well as Johnny Otis. He was known as "Vice Pres" because of the influence of Lester Young on his playing. Quinchette recorded with small groups in the 1950s. He left music in the 1960 to work in the electronics industry but returned to recordings and live performances in the 1970s.

area, that area that was fondly referred to by the people of the thirties, forties, and fifties as "The Avenue." While Central Avenue itself, first at 11th Street and Central Avenue, and later and more importantly, at 42nd and Central, was the heartland and the main focus of the activity, other streets and areas were vital parts of the Central Avenue movement also. They included, Washington Boulevard, San Pedro Street, Santa Barbara Boulevard (now Martin Luther King Boulevard), Western Avenue, Avalon Boulevard, Adams Boulevard, Jefferson Avenue, and in the southeastern or Watts area, 103rd Street, Imperial Highway, and Wilmington Avenue.

Any attempt to trace the original roots of a particular form of Black American music requires flowing back in time and place to the Deep South. If this book were to be an attempt at a chronologically and scientifically complete examination of the African American cultural tree, it would require the input of historians, anthropologists, archivists, musicologists, and so on, with emphasis on the African motherland.

The purpose of this book, however, shall be to present the personal memories and photographs of people who were in and of the Black community and to afford the reader a firsthand, insider's view of what it was like during that fascinating time when Los Angeles was giving birth to its rhythm and blues music style. And I also want to bring things up to the present, to show what has and has not changed since those days.

Rhythm and blues music, it should be noted, did not incubate in Los Angeles in a vacuum. Every Black community in America that had a night club, a church choir, a jazz musician, a gospel group, or a blues singer contributed directly or indirectly to the L.A. music scene. Other important American cities with large African American populations were also centers of rhythm and blues development: New Orleans, Memphis, Chicago, Detroit, and New York, for instance. What set Los Angeles apart was the fact that Black performers throughout the country, and especially in the South, perceived Los Angeles as a kind of promised land, with many glamorous night spots, sunny weather, and a more benign form of racism than in most American cities.

The list of early African American musical artists who reflected and defined the Black culture of Los Angeles is long and distinguished. The fact that so many of the key players have passed away gave me a special sense of urgency about this project. Given enough time there would be no one left to document authentically the era, no one left to interview.

Almost without exception, the old-timers of the period display a sadness when comparing the early days to the present time. "We had so much then," Jimmy Witherspoon laments, "We had so many nice night spots . . . places like the Last Word and the Down Beat . . . and full-scale cabarets too like The Club Alabam and Shepp's Playhouse . . . big ballrooms such as Joe Morris's Plantation . . . blues incubators like the Barrelhouse in Watts and after-hours spots all over the place . . . Johnny Cornish's Double Vee, Alex Lovejoy's Big Legged Chicken, Brother's, Stuff Crouch's Back Stage, Black Dot McGee's, The Jungle Room, and Jack's Basket Room. And sharp restaurants like Ivy's Chicken Shack . . . wow! No wonder so much great music came out of Central Avenue. But it's all gone now . . . nothing left but crack and hardship."

PART 1

✴

CENTRAL AVENUE
BREAKDOWN

✴

Remembering the Avenue

Since the seventies Johnny Otis has conducted a weekly radio program broadcast on listener-sponsored Pacifica Radio stations in Los Angeles, Berkeley, and Fresno, California. The following three conversations about Central Avenue come from that show.

A Conversation with
JAMES TOLBERT, attorney
LIL CUMBER, theatrical agent/writer
BOB BARBER, bailbondsman
CAL BAILEY, artist
JOHNNY OTIS, host

JAMES TOLBERT: "The thirties and forties on Central Avenue were magical times and very important to me."

BOB BARBER: "Yes, and Los Angeles was where all the action . . . all the activity went on in one area . . . Central Avenue. The only other city I know of that was similar was Denver, Colorado."

JOHNNY OTIS: "With the Five Points district."

B.B.: "That's it, Five Points."

J.T.: "In the old days, everyone lived one or two blocks off Central Avenue. One way or another. Either over to Hooper, or over to Naomi. You'd say tailor, and everyone immediately thought of Mr. King the tailor . . . there was one tailor. Now, there were a lot of preachers, but one man stands out in my memory, Reverend Clayton Russell. He was so far ahead of his time."

LIL CUMBER: "A man who really cared about people."

J.T.: "And a preacher with a vision and a program."

J.O.: "He was into standing up for human rights and civil rights before it was popular to do so."

B.B.: "Yeah, in those days, our own people . . . some of them . . . got nervous if you talked about standing up for your rights."

J.O.: "When I first started our Landmark Community Church, Clayton had a popular radio broadcast from his church. He would actually bring me on the broadcast and promote the idea of my ministry and our church."

L.C.: "We don't have enough of that kind of feeling in the community now. There are some things I feel very badly about. I don't think we have enough self-pride. Because we should have gone back and developed our old community and make it great like the Japanese and other people have done with their areas."

B.B.: "Central Avenue was one of the most outstanding places I've ever seen. Central Avenue was much more than I ever thought I'd be able to enjoy in this world. I was raised in a very small town in Texas, and when I hit Los Angeles as a young guy, it was like heaven to me. Now, I agree with Lil that we should lift our own community and not run off as soon as we get a few dollars. I don't feel our progress has been in the right direction. I believe in staying at home and cleaning up my own backyard. Look at Koreatown and Little Tokyo and those places. Those people are happy . . . those people have a lot of togetherness."

L.C.: "We have to learn to be that way. We have to develop self-pride. I'm not

With Joe Louis and friends at the Club Alabam on Central Avenue, circa 1952. Left to right: Johnny Otis, John Thomas (boxer), unknown woman, Joe Louis, Leonard Reed (entertainer), and Chalky Wright (boxer). (By permission of Tom Reed)

Sweet N Hot basketball team, circa 1944. Team included musicians Calvin Jackson, Charles Mingus, Lee Young, and Carmen Leary (top row l-r) and Maxwell Davis and Leonard Reed (bottom row l-r). Photo courtesy/Leonard Reed/Tom Reed Collection.

saying you've got to stay in the community, but we've got to contribute and care about it."

B.B.: "Now, I'm not a Muslim, and I don't say I'll ever be a Muslim, but there's one thing I gotta say. They've taught their youngsters to keep a clean collar around their necks . . . they done that."

J.O.: "You got that right!"

L.C.: "And their hair well-groomed."

B.B.: "And they've taught them some discipline and togetherness."

CAL BAILEY: "Father Divine gave us some of that, too."

L.C.: "I know this is controversial, but we've been welfare oriented too long."

J.T.: "Controversy don't bother me, but I think we're getting away from Central Avenue of the thirties and forties."

B.B.: "Well, it all ties in, you know."

J.T.: "Yes, that's true enough, but let's talk about the Florence Mills Theatre and the Bill Robinson and the Clark Hotel . . . Doctor Henderson and people like that."

J.O.: "Okay, Jimmy, tell us about Doctor Henderson."

Johnny Otis with Dizzy Gillespie (left), John Pettigrew, and Earl Warren, 1947. At this time, Gillespie's work with Charlie Parker established important new directions for jazz.

J.T.: "I knew Doctor Henderson down at the Clark Hotel when I used to wash dishes there. One day, Doctor Henderson looked at me, just after I had goofed somehow, and he said, 'nobody's home.' All the people fell out laughing, but I didn't know what he meant. He was talking about me and my trifling ways. When I caught on, I just prayed he didn't complain about me to my grandfather because he'd call up my Uncle Lee and tell him, 'Come over and whip this boy,' and Uncle Lee would gladly come right over and accommodate him. I guess he felt it was good exercise to keep his arms in shape for playing the drums. But, you know, you had a climate of discipline in the thirties and forties. You didn't dare miss school, for instance. And we had a strong church influence. Another thing comes to mind where our church activity was concerned. It was before World War II, and I was attending Reverend Grant Harris's Zion Hill and we couldn't wait 'til Sunday to see what kind of new, fantastic hats Gertrude Gipson and her sister Lillian would wear."

J.O.: "Jimmy, you are part of a very musical family . . . a famous musical family. Your uncle, Lee Young, was a fine drummer, and his brother, your uncle, Lester Young, was not only the president of the tenor sax but in my opinion the guiding spirit of modern jazz. How do you remember Prez?"

J.T.: "Well, he was so busy on the road that we didn't see him that often. Uncle Bubba, as we called him, was mostly symbolic in our family. I remember the whole family would gather around the radio to hear him broadcast with Count Basie. And we knew when it was Herschel Evans or Buddy Tate playing.

When Prez would take a solo with that haunting tone we'd all holler, 'that's Uncle Bubba!' But Uncle Lee was my personal hero. He would take me to the fights and to ball games, and sometimes, while he was shaving, getting ready to go on a gig, he would ask me challenging questions, and if I got the answer right, I'd get a quarter. And, let me tell you, a quarter in 1935 was a big deal to a kid."

With Gerald Wilson in Los Angeles, 1946. Wilson distinguished himself as an excellent trumpet player with the Jimmie Lunceford Band between 1939 and 1942, and led his own band in Los Angeles in the 1940s. He went on to play with Count Basie and Dizzy Gillespie. His composition "Viva Tirado" became a hit song for the Los Angeles band El Chicano in 1970. Johnny's son Shuggie is married to Gerald's daughter Terry.

J.O.: "Lester Young's mother and father, your grandparents, lived next door to our Black musicians' union building on Central Avenue. I used to see you there when we were youngsters. It must have been wonderful to have been a part of a family band that included Lester Young."

J.T.: "By the time I started playing in the band. Uncle Bubba (Lester) was gone to the majors, so to speak. You played drums on a lot of records with Lester's band, Johnny, so, you probably saw him more than I did during the forties. But my memories of the family band are vivid. If you think Illinois Jacquet and Big Jay McNeely were sensational showmen, then you should've seen my cousins Boots and Sport in the Young family band. In fact, Lester developed the habit of holding his horn up high just so it would appear that he too was into showmanship. And, get this, they tell me that my aunt Erma could outblow Lester at one time."

J.O.: "The idea of anyone outblowing Lester Young boggles my imagination."

J.T.: "Well, mine too, but that's what the family members say. And Aunt Erma was more than just a sax tooter . . . she was a very popular dancer and comedienne in Los Angeles years ago. And here's something I remember about the old Local 767 building next door. Johnny, you remember baritone sax man, "Big Boy" Davidson?"

J.O.: "Yeah, he doubled as the janitor at the building."

J.T.: "Right, well a week didn't pass that he didn't lock himself out of the building by mistake. This was always late at night, and he'd come knocking at our door, and I'd have to jump from the roof of our house, to the union roof, go through the attic window, and come around and let him in. It's really a wonder I didn't kill myself!"

Central Avenue Revisited

Conversation with
BUDDY COLLETTE, saxophonist/band leader
DOOTSIE WILLIAMS, ex-trumpeter/band leader, owner of Dootone Records
JOHNNY OTIS, host

DOOTSIE WILLIAMS: "In the days before we had much experience with agents or managers things were different. I remember I lived at 95th and Central, and Joe Turner and Pete Johnson lived at 99th. I raised a lot of chickens, and Joe Turner was crazy about chicken, this is way before Colonel's Kentucky Fried, ha, ha. But Joe Turner was a guy who could really wring a chicken's neck. I couldn't do it, but Joe could wring a chicken's neck, and that chicken would fly about twenty feet in the air, and when it came down it would start walkin' and jumpin' and dancin', and we'd take 'em in the kitchen and cook 'em, and me and Joe and Pete Johnson'd have a feast! Dan Grissom, Jimmy Lunceford's ex-singer and sax man lived right next door to Joe Turner out in Watts, and he ran an after-hours joint there. That's where Joe used to sing "Drink hearty but stay in your party," because anytime a guy came in there and started looking at someone else's woman, all hell could break loose!"

JOHNNY OTIS: "The Harlem Renaissance has been well documented on film and in print, and so on, but our own history of the Black community here in Los Angeles—and I don't mean just in music and having fun knocking off chickens but the total community—was a marvel in those days. And it has not been recorded in any meaningful way, and suddenly, in the past few years, writers and filmmakers have begun coming around and asking questions."

BUDDY COLLETTE: I think they're finding, more and more, that there was so much that was skipped over, and there are not too many of us around to even tell the story. So naturally, it's becoming more important all the time."

D.W.: "We had good writers, but they couldn't get published . . . I mean, by any major publishers. A lot of people doing a lot of good things but no way to preserve the history of it."

J.O.: "We sure had good writers, and a lot of them too—people like Abie Robinson, Almena Lomax, Lil Cumber, Joe "Smoke Rings" Harris, Stanley Robertson, Pat Alexander, Wendell Green, Gertrude Gibson, Colonel Leon Washington, Mrs. Charlotta Bass, Brad Pie, Jr., Herman Hill, but they seldom, if ever, saw the light of day in the mainstream press . . . that is to say, in the white press, in actual book form."

D.W.: "They couldn't find a publisher."

B.C.: "But there was so much going on . . . even they couldn't cover it all. Now, here's the three of us . . . we were there . . . we don't know all of the same stories, but we have memories of a lot of different things that happened. It's true they were writing for the Black press . . . the *Eagle*, the *Tribune*, the *Sentinel*, and all that . . . but never published by the big publishers . . . and that's why I think it's an untapped source."

D.W.: "Almena had the *Tribune*, Colonel Washington had the *Sentinel*."

J.O.: "Mrs. Bass had the *Eagle*, then later, Attorney Loren Miller had it,

Johnny Otis and Dootsie Williams, 1955. Dootise Williams recorded Big Joe Turner, Redd Foxx, the Penguins, and others on his DooTone Label.

Ivy Anderson (1905–1949) with the Johnny Otis Orchestra at the Cricket Club in Los Angeles, 1947. Born in Gilroy, California, Anderson danced and sang in Harlem's Cotton Club, toured with the Sissle and Blake musical "Shuffle Along," and sang with bands fronted by Earl "Fatha" Hines, and Duke Ellington. She operated a restaurant in Los Angeles in the mid-1940s and made her last recording in 1946 with a band that included Willie Smith and Charles Mingus.

and finally Attorney Jimmy Tolbert. It was a culture within a culture here. Life was breathed into a life-style and a musical style here. I'm reminded of Charles Mingus, Sonny Criss, and yourself, Buddy."

B.C.: "Well, Johnny, I know you remember the time a group called Jazz Alive came out here and did a concert called Central Avenue Breakdown. We had a protest meeting at your church about the idea of people who weren't even around pretending to present the idea of Central Avenue on stage with mostly youngsters, and almost all-white at that. For instance, they couldn't have known about Dootsie's band."

D.W.: "Well, not too many people knew about my band."

B.C.: "Oh yes, they did. In the old days, I only lived about four or five blocks from Dootsie. In fact, my parents were close to his parents, and he was very instrumental in getting me started in music. I mean as far as being a guy who could read and everything. There was a party at your house, and my parents were there, and they said, 'Well, our son plays saxophone,' and you said, 'Well, I've got some music here.' That night my parents brought home a small trunk full of music, and the next morning I woke up, and it was like Christmas! Here's all this music—I was probably about 12 years old and had switched from piano to sax and wanted to have a band, and suddenly I had a book of 50 or 60 arrangements! Dootsie, you discarded them, but they were like gold to me 'cause if you want to be a band leader, the first thing you've gotta have is a book. I had two or three little buddies who wanted to play, and we started trying to form a band. We had one alto, and we found a trumpet player, Charlie Martin on piano, and a drummer named Minor Robinson, and there we were, a band."

J.O.: "Dootsie, I remember you coming to the Barrelhouse Club in 1948 to listen to Billy "Woodpecker" Mitchell who was doing comedy there, and you recorded Billy, Hattie Noel, and Redd Foxx; your Dootone Record label was off and running. How did you find Redd Fox?"

D.W.: "Well, first I got tired of playing trumpet and struggling with a band, and I said, 'I'm gonna have a record company.' I found Redd Foxx working at the Oasis Club on Western Avenue where he was working for $25 a night on Saturdays and Sundays. And so, I listened to this guy, and he wasn't really obscene, just naughty by those standards. But then, he was so outrageous in such a way that nobody would ever think of putting him on a record. But I thought, 'this guy can sell.' If he could shock and make such an impression that people would fall out in the aisles at him, I said, 'this will sell.' So, I took this recording I made and I played it for some church people, and they—ooh!—they just went crazy! One lady says, 'I'm going back to Texas, can you make me a copy.' And so then I went back to Redd Foxx and told him, I said, 'People would buy this. I'd like to release it.' Redd said, 'Man, nobody's gonna' take my act! If I record it they won't want to see me live. No! No!' So, the next day I see him and he's broke, and he says, 'Hey, what was that you were saying last night about recording?' I said, 'I'll give you $25 if you just let me bring my recording set and I'll record your whole act.' He says, 'Okay,' and the rest is history."

J.O.: "When you recorded that first album, Redd Foxx was working with me as an assistant on my KFOX disc jockey show. He sat there while the R&B records were spinning and drew a picture of himself dressed in Bermuda shorts."

D.W.: "Yeah, I put that drawing on the cover of his first album."

J.O.: "And then a few years passed, and you really hit the jackpot with a new R&B vocal group called Cleve Duncan and the Penguins. That's when they recorded 'Earth Angel' for you."

D.W.: "Sure, and I kinda backed into that one. I was doing demonstration records for song writers at that time. A guy would give me 100 bucks, and I would make a record of his song, right? So, I had these guys over to Ted Brinson's backyard studios. I had the Penguins doing some vocals, and they begged me, 'Please record us so we can get a release and go on the road and get famous,' and all that. They kept buggin' me 'til I said, 'Okay, what have you got?' They said, 'We got a song called 'Earth Angel' and a song called 'Hey Senorita.' Of course, 'Earth Angel' was all messed up, you know how they come to you. So I straightened it out here and straightened it out there, and, doggone, it sounded pretty good."

J.O.: "I remember you brought me 'Earth Angel' on a 78 when it was first released. I was doing a DJ show in the window of Conley's Record Rack in Watts at 111th and Wilmington. You said, 'Hey, Johnny, here's a new release. Spin it for me.' I played it. It took off and became a million seller and an all-time R&B

"Johnnie" Otis, his drums, and his orchestra play at the Orpheum Theatre in Los Angeles, 1946.

classic love song. The Penguins got their wish, fame, and traveling on the road, and now, you were successful in R&B as well as comedy records."

D.W.: "Yeah, then I got lucky with Vernon Green & the Medallions with 'Buick 59' and 'The Letter' and Don Julian and the Meadowlarks with 'Heaven and Paradise,' and a lot of stuff. In the meantime, Redd Foxx was selling plenty albums, too. But, you know, when people start talking about Central Avenue bands they forget there were more than just Mingus, Lionel Hampton, Johnny Otis, and Gerald Wilson."

J.O.: "Oh, God, yeah! There were many fine bands stretching back into the thirties—Paul Howard, Curtis Mosby's Blue Blowers, Edythe Turnham's Dixie Aces, the Woodman's Family band."

B.C.: "That's right, and don't forget George Brown, Les Hite, and Al Adams."

D.W.: "And Floyd Ray, Happy Johnson, and Peppy Prince, too."

J.O.: "How did you start in the L.A. scene as a musician, Buddy?"

B.C.: "Well, actually, I lived in Watts and some of my first experiences were of that part of the Los Angeles area. I remember Charles Mingus as a classical cellist and his sisters Grace and Vivian, one played piano and the other played violin. Even before I became friends with Mingus, I knew, as most of us did, that he was a wild person and all the trouble he would get into. Somebody said, 'Someday you'll see this guy. He's fat and bowlegged and usually acting weird.' Once I met him on the corner of 96th and Compton, and there he was with this shoe shine box. But it was three feet tall. Now, I used to shine shoes as a kid, too, but never with a contraption like that. I said, 'Hey, you're Charles Mingus, aren't you?' From that day we were friends. I told him, 'Too bad you don't play string bass instead of cello 'cause you could be in my band.' I was

Backstage at the Million Dollar Theatre, Los Angeles, 1947. From left, Johnny Otis, Phyllis Otis, James Ricks (whose bass vocals provided the distinctive sound for the Ravens and who had eleven Top Twenty rhythm and blues hit songs between 1948 and 1952), holding Janice Otis.

big-timin'. But before then, I played with the Bledsoe Brothers' band. Ralph and Riley Bledsoe who are both doctors now; they were twins from the Watts area. In the Jordan High band, music teacher Mr. Lippy had them both playing tuba, marching right up front. In their own band, one played trombone and the other tuba. String bass was just coming in strong, and Mingus used to laugh at them and say, 'Hey, you can't slap a horn!' I played in their band before I got my own. Their father, old Doctor Bledsoe, was a very strict and stern man. On their nineteenth birthday, they had a party but were not allowed to invite girls. There we were, seventeen-, eighteen-, and nineteen-year old guys and no ladies. Crosby Lewis and Minor and I played in their band, but their father got so heavy-handed that we quit, and I started my own band. About this time, we started going into L.A. and hanging out at the 54th Street Drug Store at 54th and Central. This was a very cool thing to do because all the older cats hung around there too. Sometimes, I'd see Mingus there. I'd be glad to see him but was always touchy around him."

J.O.: "Yeah, Mingus was nerve-wracking to be around, because you never knew what he might do from one minute to the next. One day, the two of us were walking down the tracks across the street from the Watts Towers, where the Red Car used to run in Watts. We met three mean-looking dudes coming the other way. They were older guys, in their forties, big, muscular cats, and as they came by us, one of them said, 'Get outa the way old ugly, bow-legged boy!' And Mingus exploded on those three guys and went to swingin' and sluggin', and I said, 'Oh, no, no!' because I could see us getting stomped. But, you know what? He punched them so fast and so hard that they broke and ran, and Mingus kept growling to himself, 'grr . . . grrr!' All that energy and that wildness that was in him, he was able to translate that into some spectacular music."

D.W.: "In that era we're talking about, there was discipline in the bands, sharp uniforms and correct behavior."

J.O.: "And the older men and women rode herd on us to make sure we didn't goof."

B.C.: "But we've lost much of that. When the older cats told us, 'Hey, young blood, you gotta do this, you gotta do that, it was a valuable thing, just like correct home training from your parents.

You know, the actual geographical area we're dealing with stretched from Watts, through greater L.A. and up into Pasadena. There were good Pasadena musicians like Skeets Lundy, Butter and Walt Ellis, Robert Forliece, and Bob and George Brown."

D.W.: "When we talk about racial boundaries within L.A. County in the thirties and forties, you have to remember that Blacks were not allowed south of Slauson for many years."

B.C.: "Around 58th Street or around Slauson, that was about it, wasn't it?"

D.W.: "That was it until you go way south, all the way to Watts at about 94th Street. I remember a Black family had the nerve, the audacity, to move in at 92nd Street, and the whites gave them a terrible time."

J.O.: "Years ago, I heard old-timers say that the racial demarcation line ran straight down the middle of Central Avenue. In other words, Blacks could live and have businesses on the east side of the Avenue but not on the west."

D.W.: "That's right, the east side was blocked out. As the years went by, small sections, here and there fell into Black hands. When I first came here, Blacks could live at 5th and Central up to 12th. Then we had to jump to about where the Lincoln Theatre used to be. Then to Jefferson and Central and finally to 42nd and Central where the Club Alabam and the Dunbar Hotel were. It was just a series of little strips."

Johnny Otis and Redd Foxx, 1956.

J.O.: "The concept of Watts and Central Avenue can be taken to mean two different places, but, in fact, Central Avenue runs from downtown L.A. to and through Watts. So, although Central Avenue exists outside of Watts, Watts is always part of Central Avenue."

B.C.: "When we say Watts we're saying Central Avenue. It's all tied in together."

D.W.: "We jumped over the white enclaves to get to our homes if we lived in Watts and were coming from the downtown area. Drove right through them, actually."

J.O.: "Yeah, and fast, too, sometimes." [laughs]

D.W.: "With automobiles and the Watts Local and with that streetcar that would go from way up from L.A. City College and run all the way down to Manchester and Central Avenue. Then, you had to get off and walk."

J.O.: "Yeah, and Manchester is about 85th Street. So, if you lived around 103rd Street you had a long walk."

D.W.: "Yeah, and you were walking through the white district until you came to 95th Street."

B.C.: "I used to have dreams about that, about walking through no-man's-land, and late at night, too."

D.W.: "Social conditions were terrible at that time. But our Black culture was in many ways in better shape then. I don't want to say that the old times were better times."

J.O.: "That's what all old folks say." [laughs]

D.W.: "Well, I won't say it was better, but it was different."

B.C.: "I won't say it was better either, but there's a lot we can learn from our early culture. Some of our young artists today pick up an instrument, learn three chords and two scales and get lucky with a record, and feel they have reached the artistic heights. But if you're so great, and you've reached your full potential at eighteen or twenty, then where is there to go or grow at thirty or forty? We learned a lot when we went on the road with the old bands, all that musical experience and that life experience too. We had mature mentors, older musicians to help us get all the training we could. Today, it's all kids together, and something really gets lost in the process."

J.O.: "In the early days, you were either on Decca, Columbia, or Victor doing big band swing, or you were Big Bill Broonzy, Peetie Wheatstraw, or Leadbelly recording country blues on the 'race' labels. It wasn't until Black record independents like the Rene Brothers, Jack Lauderdale, and you, Dootsie, that the R&B artists and our local jazz players got a chance to record."

D.W.: "Well, if we wait for whites to promote the Black issue, the Black concept, the Black viewpoint, we'll be waiting a long time."

J.O.: "You know, we don't have many young Blacks dealing with the traditional Black viewpoint. I don't mean the synthetic Black viewpoint promoted on today's television or the often arrogant, warlike, and obscene Black pop records we hear so much of. I'm afraid we haven't preserved the traditional Black social wisdom. Our kids don't know how we are always in danger of disaster because of racism."

D.W.: "At one time, we could easily recognize racism because it was so blatant. But today it is so smooth and sneaky that our younger generation of Blacks is lulled into a sense of false fantasy. Hell, they don't even know they're being discriminated against, it is so polished and perfected."

B.C.: "I wish I could say I have seen things really change for the better in the country, but I'm afraid that in spite of certain improvements here and there for Black people, that the total picture is worse now than it was many years ago. In the thirties in the Watts area where I grew up, we had whites, Japanese, Mexican, and Blacks living in the neighborhoods, and it worked. We got along fine. What did happen was, at a certain point, some families could get better jobs and move to another area."

J.O.: "Did this cause an all-Black community to develop?"

B.C.: "Yes, in a way. I mean, it didn't happen all at once. During and after the war, it happened. But during the earlier time, everyone got along, and it had great educational value for all the various ethnic groups of the area. The idea that my ace buddy could be a Japanese or a white kid, or whatever, you know, it was great. We were in school together, having lunch together. So, the people who were there were there because they didn't have a lot of money or the property was affordable, but those ten or fifteen years that I remember were very meaningful for people getting to know one another as people, so, we had a thing that we rarely see today. That was a period when it looked hopeful."

D.W.: "Well, as a kid I thought, hey, I can be anything I want to be. That's what they taught us in school, and I believed it. You know, be president, governor, head of a major corporation, but it really wasn't true at all at that time, and it's not true now."

B.C.: "That's my whole point. It wasn't true then, and it may be even harder now."

D.W.: "You know, if Duke Ellington came along now he wouldn't be a success. I'm sure of it."

B.C.: "Yes, because at the time he came through, it worked. People were tuned in to that excellent artistry. A good example of this is pianist, composer, and conductor Calvin Jackson. A few months before he passed, I was at his home in San Diego, and he showed me all these marvelous musical scores, twenty-five-, thirty-five-piece works, powerful stuff. And he was hoping, and we can understand this, that he was going to be able to get his work performed on TV and the concert halls. I didn't have the heart to tell him what I thought about his chances."

J.O.: "Now here was a truly fine artist, steeped in the classical tradition. He

Bardu Ali and Johnny Otis at the Barrelhouse Club, 1948.

Johnny Otis with Marvin and Johnny, 1955. Marvin Phillips sang duets with Jesse Belvin as well as with Johnny Perry. In the early 1950s, Marvin and Johnny's "Tick Tock," and "Cherry Pie" hit the charts.

was at MGM while still in his early twenties. But in the eighties, after a lifetime of being left out, he was languishing on the shelf."

D.W.: "What would have happened if he were born white?"

B.C.: "I'm sure he would've been a successful man in the Hollywood music world—movies, television, and on the concert stage, too."

J.O.: "He wasn't some eccentric talent with bad habits who turned people off. He was a very nice guy, a gentleman."

B.C.: "Long ago, he was Georgie Stoll's assistant at MGM, and André Prévin was a notch below that. Later, André Prévin became the conductor of the L.A. Philharmonic, and of course, with his fine talent he deserved it. But Calvin wasn't able to work in Los Angeles. He gained much fame and recognition in Canada but not in his own country."

A Grand Time

Conversation with
PATSY HUNTER, show producer/choreographer
CLARENCE "FRENCHY" LANDRY, dancer/member of the High Hatters
CAROLINE HARLSON, vocalist
JOHNNY OTIS, host

JOHNNY OTIS: "Frenchy, let me ask you a question. What was it like to be young, gifted, Black, and part of a great dancing trio in the Central Avenue heyday?"

FRENCHY LANDRY: "It made you feel like you were a king. Especially since I had so many schoolmates who followed us and supported us. And to be performing with Basie, Ellington, Lunceford, well, I have to say that was the best thing that ever happened to me."

J.O.: "I saw you at the World's Fair in San Francisco in 1939, and I thought, what wonderful dancers! Lord, please let me be part of that world! My prayers were answered a few years later when I had the band at the Club Alabam and you and Vernard and Eudell were featured on the show and Patsy was the producer."

PATSY HUNTER: "What a grand time that was!"

F.L.: "Oh, there is so much to remember and so much history. I'm glad to be passing some of these memories on."

J.O.: "Patsy, we never know, sometimes, what a deep impression we make on each other. I remember in 1943, down on Central Avenue, when I was just a little upstart, playing drums with Harlan Leonard's Kansas City Rockets, and you were the producer of the shows at the Club Alabam. So, anyhow, I'd been there a while, trying to learn to play the floor shows, and you were always giving me good advice. For instance, you told me if I ever got lost or confused about what was happening to just roll on the snare drum until I found my way."

P.H.: "Ha ha, yes, do you remember that?"

J.O.: "I'll never forget it. But one night you really laid it on me. You called me aside and said, 'Listen, son, you tell me that your ambition is to be a bandleader someday. Well, don't take this wrong, but the first thing you gotta do is come outa that zoot suit. You idolize Duke Ellington and Count Basie, you don't see them wearing zoot suits.' I said, 'Cab Calloway wears 'em.' You said, 'On the stage . . . not on the street!'

P.H.: "Well, I felt you should prepare yourself to do what you wanted to do. I didn't want to hurt your feelings, you know."

Etta James was an aspiring sixteen-year-old singer when Johnny Otis discovered her in San Francisco in the mid-1950s. She went on to become a big star.

J.O.: "I knew you were just being helpful, but it embarrassed me. In fact, it embarrassed me so good that I went out and got myself some new clothes."

CAROLINE HARLSON: "You can't beat having a good role model and some positive discipline."

F.L.: "That's something we sure had, even if we were living in a world of discrimination. Another thing stands out in my memory, Madame Hoodah, the lady who made the costumes for the performers at the Club Alabam."

C.H.: "Oh, my, you've got a good memory, Frenchy."

Johnny Otis running equipment at Dig Records, 1955.

F.L.: "I'm talking about Madame Hoodah. She was a costumer we could depend on for great outfits."

P.H.: "If she promised us twelve costumes by noon Thursday, we had them by noon Thursday."

F.L.: "And they were always original, and fabulous!"

C.H.: "And all the great musicians, singers, dancers, they all migrated to Central Avenue from all across the country. Here they came by the dozens to get a taste of that Central Avenue and to try to be discovered."

P.H.: "And they all stayed at the Dunbar Hotel, 'cause there was nowhere else to stay."

C.H.: "Patsy, remember how we would meet the buses when the bands came to town?"

P.H.: "Do I? And I remember when Fats Waller came out here to do 'Stormy Weather' and we all met him."

F.L.: "We had a prince come into the Dunbar Hotel, Prince Modupe. When he first came, he worked at the hotel as a bell hop, and then he went home to Africa."

P.H.: "And when he came back he had this big group of servants with him."

F.L.: "All those trunks full of clothes and stuff. He said, 'I went back home and my father was now king, so, I'm back to see my friends, but this time not as a bell hop.' And I remember when Father Divine took over the whole Dunbar Hotel."

J.O.: "Remember how much meals were at the Father Divine Restaurant in those days?"

F.L.: "Yeah, twenty five cents."

C.H., P.H., J.O. [in unison]: "Fifteen cents!"

F.L.: "Right, and twenty five cents if you wanted dessert, and a nickel more if you wanted a shoe shine."

J.O.: "And if you were hungry and didn't have any money at all?"

F.L.: "If you were broke and you said, 'Thank You, Father,' the meal was free."

C.H.: "Don't forget, 'Peace It's Truly Wonderful.'"

F.L.: "'Thank You, Father, Peace It's Truly Wonderful,' and they'd feed you free."

P.H.: "Times have really changed. I was thinking, when I was doing the shows at the Alabam and elsewhere, we changed the shows every two weeks. Now, in Vegas, Tahoe, and Atlantic City shows go on and on and on."

Johnny Otis, Big Mama Thornton, and Little Arthur Matthews in Birmingham, Alabama, 1954.

F.L.: "Now, I'm gonna take you way back. Patsy, before you started doing the shows, I ran the shows at the club. Curtis Mosby had closed it (he opened it up again later). But now, two Italian brothers, Ben and Pete Rizzotta had it. I had Herb Jeffries on my shows: Lillian Randolph, Crip Heard, Willie Lewis, and Francis Neely. Big Time Crip Heard, the great one-legged dancer. The town was wide open then. You could stay open after hours or anything, you know, just as long as you took care of a few people, you know, grease a few palms."

C.H.: "There are some things I wish we could go back to. One is, a woman or a young girl could walk down Central Avenue at three o'clock in the morning with no problem of being accosted or robbed. And we could see the best of acts, hear the finest music, go to the Lincoln Theatre or the Club Alabam and see a great show. I mean with class. Walk from club to club in perfect safety. It was glamorous, and our people strived for class and they had class."

P.H.: "Not much of that left today, is there?"

F.L.: " 'Fraid not."

C.H.: "Johnny, do you remember the time we were working at the Alabam with Butterbeans and Suzie?"

J.O.: "Yeah, and they gave you a great birthday party one night."

C.H.: "Right! They knew me as a child back in Chicago. My dad was Willie Richardson, the comedian. They used to gig together."

J.O.: "Let's see, that was about 1943 and it was your birthday. Tell me, my dear, how old were you then?"

C.H.: "Well, my dear, since you are so nosy, I was about two years old then, which makes me around thirty-nine now. You were already about forty-five at the time, my dear. Ha, ha!"

[Everybody cracks up laughing.]

The Barbershop Experts on Central

Many barbershops up and down Central Avenue usually had at least one barber who was an expert on everything. In the five-chair shop where Bardu Ali and I regularly had our hair cut, there were two self-proclaimed geniuses. All day long, the discussions went on. The topics were usually music or sports, but there was plenty of talk on international affairs, politics, religion, medicine, mechanics, or anything at all. If you were interested in a fast shave or haircut, the "Le Petit Deluxe Barbershop and Process Parlor" was a poor choice, because as the discussions became heated debates, all five barbers were known to gather in the aisle, combs and razors waving in the air, as they shouted one other down.

"Jack Johnson would've killed Joe Louis in the first round, and that goes for Dempsey, too!"

"B-u-u-u-l shit, Dempsey maybe, But not Mighty Joe . . . one, two . . . one, two . . . MOP! . . . Joe drops that shit on him . . . BAM! Jack Johnson's lyin' on his big ass, OUT!"

On world affairs: "Man, what you talkin' about? Stalin ain't gonna fuck with Uncle Sam. He's too slick for that."

"Oh yeah? Lissen, that bad motherfucker'll fuck with the devil. Look at all them cats with them long coats and them fur hats on. They ain't playin', baby."

Sometimes the shoe shine man was brought into the debate as a kind of final authority. "Hey, Billy, tell this cat something, man. You know the U.S. is ready for their communist asses."

Little fat Billy would step into the fray with the air of a military scholar. "I know a guy works at Fort Ord says it's a top secret, but the army got a gas make you lose your body fluids within ten minutes. One

Jimmy Witherspoon and the Jackson Brothers Band, Watts South Health Council Show, 1952. Born in Arkansas, Jimmy Witherspoon moved to Los Angeles in 1935. He sang with the Jay McShann Band between 1944 and 1947 and had five Top Forty rhythm and blues hits between 1949 and 1952.

little whiff, all the Russians is washed up. Them communists know that. They ain't crazy. They ain't gonna fuck with America, Jim."

The owner of Le Petit was a man from New Orleans of Creole background. He called everyone Coozahn, and everyone called him Coozahn. His station was the first barber chair facing the big front window. Behind him, on the wall was a phone. Coozahn's main business was bookin' horses. No one used that phone but Coozahn. The phone rang constantly. If you wound up in Coozahn's chair for a haircut, you needed plenty of time and patience. From time to time, Coozahn would send Shoe Shine Billy around back where Coozahn's wife, Pearl, kept track of the booking business.

One day Coozahn was giving me a haircut, and the phone rang. "Just a minute," Coozahn told the caller. "Billy, go back and see who's the winner in the third." Billy came back and said, "Do Right Mama is the winner. Coozahn passed the information on to the caller and went back to cutting my hair. Old man Willis, one of the barbershop regulars was sitting on the bench by the shoe shine stand looking through his racing form. "Ain't no Do Right Mama runnin' in the third," he grumbled. "What?" Coozahn said. "Let me see that. Ain't this a bitch! Billy, you no reading, motherfucker, the horse's name is Do Re Me!"

Slappy White and Redd Foxx performing a comedy routine with the Johnny Otis Show in 1947.

None of the barbers or the regulars at Le Petit were musicians, but when musicians came in, their presence usually touched off great debates on blues and jazz. None of the crew were nuclear physicists either, but that didn't deter the resident walking encyclopedias.

"Now, you take the molecule. It's the smallest piece of anything that retains its original characteristics." That's Smitty in chair three talking. Actually, he was a very learned man. In the cabinet behind his station, was a row of dictionaries and reference volumes. Any statement, on any subject brought an instant response from Jordan who loved to argue. And even if he didn't know beans about the subject at hand, it wouldn't matter. He'd simply come up with pseudo-facts or hocus pocus. This would inflame Smitty and send him rushing to his bookshelf.

The barber shop operated as a mini-theatre. Performances every day except Sunday. The regular hanger-ons and the customers loved every minute. Coozahn loved it too. It was good for business. Those who gathered for the fun were bound to place a bet or get a haircut sooner or later. "All right! Hold it down a minute, let me take this call," Coozahn would shout. As soon as Coozahn hung up, the show resumed.

The subjects that came up most often were sports and music. Stuff like molecules and atomic particles were okay for a minute, but blues singers' sexual exploits and sports star scandals were preferred. Often, Billy knew how to get the boring stuff off the agenda.

"All right, now, Smitty, check this out. How can a molecule be the littlest something when anybody who been to school knows that an atom is the smallest. Ain't that right, Billy?"

"Damn right, but lissen Jordan, scientifically speakin', a fart is the sharpest thing in the world 'cause it can go through your pants without makin' a hole. Haw, haw, haw! And, talkin' 'bout farts, how about that ole fart, George Washington, playin' trombone with Johnny Otis at the Club Alabam. He gotta be pushing seventy! Hey, Johnny, how old is he?"

"Oh, I guess about in his forties."

"Sh-e-e-e-eit! I saw that nigger playin' with Louis Armstrong in 1929, and he looked like he was forty then!"

"Aw, hell no, Jordan, that was J.C. Higgenbottom. You got the shit all backwards."

Once, while I was waiting for a chair to open up, Smitty announced that he had inside information proving Dinah Washington was a devil worshipper. Jordan, who was without education or refinement, would think nothing of dreaming up something outrageous, no matter how derogatory, about a prominent person just to gain the spotlight.

Johnny Otis plays vibes at the Nite Life Club, in Los Angeles, California, 1956.

Smitty, with all his sharpness, would allow himself to get sucked into Jordan's nonsense.

"How can you say this about Dinah! This is the fine woman who came out of the church in Chicago to become our Queen of the juke-boxes. Do you think for a minute that Lionel Hampton would hire a satanic cultist as his featured singer?"

"I don't know about that, but she sure is a devil worshipper 'cause a cat who used to work for her saw her lightin' all these black candles."

"You're degrading the name of a great lady."

"Great lady? You ever heard the bitch talk? Every other word is cussin' and swearin'!"

In the middle of this great debate, Coozahn got a phone call. He dropped the hair process job he was working on to take the call. Something had gone wrong because Coozahn snatched his apron off and ran out the door. In the early days, hair straightening was a process in-

A sensation as a child gospel singer in the 1930s, Dinah Washington (1924–1963) become a revered vocalist among jazz, blues, and popular music fans. She recorded in Los Angeles with the Lionel Hampton Orchestra and appeared frequently at the Tiffany Club.

volving strong lyes. Once the creamy lye solution was applied to one's well-lubricated scalp, there was a limit to how long this mixture could be left on before you had to wash it out with lots of water. The alternative was great pain and burned bald spots.

The classic case of what can happen if the lye is too strong or left on the scalp too long, is Eddie Cleanhead Vinson. As a young man, Eddie used some too-strong hair straightener and wound up with all his hair burned off. His hair eventually grew back, but by then, Eddie realized he had a great gimmick, and "Cleanhead" was born. To the day he passed away, Eddie shaved his head bald.

Coozahn's neglected customer who had been dozing in the chair as his hair was being done, woke up with a great scream and crashed through the barbershop to the rest room where he stuck his head in the toilet and kept flushing.

PART 2

✳

RHYTHM AND BLUES

✳

Curley and Leona's Party

Back in the late thirties, just around the corner from my home in Berkeley, lived two young women named Curley and Leona. I was a teenager then, as were Curley, Leona, and most of my friends and running buddies. One evening, my number one bosom buddy Rudy Jordan and I went to a backyard party at Curley and Leona's.

The girls had an uncle who played the trumpet. A couple of times, I had caught a glimpse or him sitting in his room practicing his horn. On this evening as we passed through the house toward the backyard, I paused to watch him play and to listen. About forty, thick-set and sitting ram rod straight in his chair, he glanced up and said, "Come on in, son." I stepped into the room and he continued playing. He had a music stand set up in front of him, but he stopped the scales and exercises on the paper and treated me to a little concert of riffs and melodies. This music he was playing was so different from the bottom-line barrelhouse stuff we played with Count Otis Matthews's band. It was no less Black than what we did with the West Oakland House Rockers, and it contained flashes of pungent blues phrases, but there was a unique elegance here . . . an element of sophistication.

What I was hearing was African American musical artistry lifted to its loftiest stage. In other words, so-called jazz. In later years, as I recruited players for my band, I remembered this man who possessed that critical balance between sophistication and heart. If a musician was all heart and soul with limited technical ability and no conceptual jazz sophistication, he or she could certainly be a fine artist in the traditional blues field where another form of subtle sophistication was required (witness Muddy Waters, Lightnin' Hopkins, or Memphis Minnie), but they were usually not equipped to function in a big modern swing band. Players who could span the gap, such as T-Bone Walker, Ray Charles, and Danny Barker, were rare exceptions. Pure country blues players were not often found in big modern swing ensembles, even though it was they who created the very foundation and essence of all popular Black music. Without the rich African American culture, without the genuine, nurtured-in-the-south, pure Black blues feeling, jazz is empty, and to me, meaningless. This authentic Black blues cultural element is the reason the Black bands were superior to the white bands. Many Black players may not have had the music lessons, the new musical instruments, and the technique of the whites, but we had that feeling. The white boys thought they had it. Or, at least, they acted as if they thought they had it. But it was, and continues to be, all copy-cat bullshit. Very rarely, there are a few white players who have the feeling and can interpret Black music beautifully: Scott Hamilton, Steve Cropper, Zoot Sims, Davey Tough, Jack Teagarden, Benny Goodman . . . , but you put a bandstand full of whites together, and you come up with a Doc Severinsin or a Stan Kenton band. And no matter that they sprinkle a few token Blacks in the band, it will still be stiff and ungainly. Sometimes, a few nice soloists, but the ensemble playing lacks that sweet, soulful, bluesy phrasing.

Most good jazz players can function well in a blues or rhythm and blues setting. Preston Love, Sonny Thompson, and King Curtis are notable examples of this kind of flexibility. Dizzy Gillespie can sing and play the blues as beautifully as any traditional artist. Charlie Parker burst onto the scene playing those classic blues solos with the early Jay McShann big band, and no matter how high he soared into the stratosphere of African American artistry, with Bird it was always the precious blues elements that wrapped his blazing technique in a blanket of Black beauty.

"Hey, ain't you coming to the party?"

"Oh, Okay, Rudy, I'm comin', I was just listening to Curley and Leona's uncle playing the trumpet."

"Man, fuck a trumpet! Don't you see all these pretty little fillies out here tonight?"

"Oooh, Rudy! Who is that fine Samoan princess over there by the swing?"

"What you tryn' to be . . . facetious or sumthin? You know who that is."

"No, I don't."

"That's Phyllis Walker."

"THAT's little Phyllis Walker, from down by 61st street?"

"Yeah."

I was bowled over. In the few years since I'd seen her, Phyllis had

Johnny Otis and members of the family, fiftieth wedding anniversary party, May 2, 1991.
Photo by Tom McElheney.

grown from a cute little neighborhood kid into a beautiful young
woman.

"Hi, Phyllis."

"Hi."

"You remember me?"

"Uh, yeah, sure."

Uh oh! I don't think she remembered me, but that's okay, because at
that moment I knew I'd pursue her like a fiend. I would make sure she'd
remember me the next time . . . and the next time . . . and the next time.

Last May 2nd, we celebrated our 50th wedding anniversary. I looked
around at all our children and grandchildren gathered here at our farm,
and I whispered, "Damn, baby! We really started something back there
in Curley and Leona's backyard fifty years ago!"

Rhythm and Blues and Malcolm X

In the early forties Black entrepreneurs discovered that being a record manufacturer was not an unattainable ambition. Jack Lauderdale established the Swingtime label. Otis and Leon Rene, the songwriting brothers from New Orleans, set up Exclusive and Excelsior Records. They had enjoyed considerable success with their compositions "When The Swallows Come Back to Capistrano" and "Sleepy Time Down South" and now decided to form record labels of their own. Otis Rene signed Nat "King" Cole, Gerald Wilson, and me to his Excelsior Label, whereas Leon picked up Joe Liggins and the Honeydrippers and Charles Brown for Exclusive. Nat Cole's first effort, a song titled "I'm Lost" (written by Otis Rene), generated good record sales and was probably what attracted Capitol Records to Nat. I got lucky with my first Excelsior release as our instrumental, "Harlem Nocturne," featuring Rene Bloch on alto sax became a big hit.

Our lives were really interwoven during the Central Avenue days. Charles Brown and I had become good friends as coworkers in Bardu Ali's band at the Lincoln Theatre. As time went by, I became the bandleader of the house band at the Club Alabam, and Charles was the featured pianist/vocalist with Johnny Moore's Three Blazers. One night, during intermission at the Club Alabam, Charles stopped by to invite me to play drums on a Johnny Moore record date for Leon Rene's Exclusive Record label. Three of the sides we recorded the following day were Nat Cole-type tunes. The fourth song, "Driftin' Blues," became a sensational smash hit, and it launched the great Charles Brown's career. At first, Charles was reluctant to record "Driftin' Blues" because it was based on a gospel song his grandmother had taught him. We had a hard time convincing him that it was alright to adapt a gospel song to a blues love song. When he finally agreed, he poured his heart into the record—

Otis Rene (at right), Los Angeles record producer, with Mr. and Mrs. John Dolphin of Dolphin's of Hollywood Record Shop, circa 1945.

not in the Nat Cole manner—but in that deep and soulful style that soon had many young R&B singers trying to sound like him.

Everyone knew everyone else in those days. Although there were many thousands of African American people in Los Angeles during the Central Avenue heyday, it was, in a way, a small world. Esvan Mosby was the honorary Mayor of Central Avenue; his brother, Curtis Mosby, was the owner of the Club Alabam. Promoters Leon and Bill Heflin were presenting their annual Cavalcade of Jazz concerts at Wrigley Field. Benny Carter told us about a great and original young piano player named Errol Garner who was playing at Billy Berg's Swing Club. Charlie Parker sat in with our band at the Club Alabam, so did Miles Davis and many great players of that time. In my band were Curtis Counce on bass; Paul Quinchette and Von Streeter on tenor saxes; Preston Love, Buddy Collette, Sonny Criss, Howard Martin, Kent Pope, and Rene Bloch at various times on alto sax; Hampton Hawes, Lee Wesley Jones, and Bill Doggett on piano; a very young and very talented Ernestine Anderson was our very first girl singer; Henry Coker and Sonny "Mush-mouth" Graven on trombones. Before I formed my Club Alabam band, I played drums with the Harlan Leonard and Bardu Ali bands, plus a few short gigs with Jack McVey and Jake Porter. And what a thrill it was to play drums with Count Basie and Art Tatum, to record with Lester Young, Illinois Jacquet, and Wynonie Harris. This was awfully heady stuff for a young guy, especially when the list included childhood idols such as Basie, Prez, and Tatum. But Central Avenue was full of thrills at that time.

There were some things that were not so thrilling, however. Like the time I went with Colonel Leon Washington, the publisher of the Black weekly, *The Los Angeles Sentinel*, to picket a white store that refused to hire Black people, although it was located in the heart of the community. A big, mean-looking white cop snatched the picket sign out of my hands and shouted, "What the fuck do you think you're doing?" In those days, the word *Negro* was the acceptable term, and as I stammered, "Well, Negro people are not being treated fairly. . . ." He circled around behind me and kicked me in the butt so hard I saw stars! The pain and the abject humiliation frustrated me so that I started to go crazy. Colonel Washington ran up and threw his arms around me and whispered hoarsely, "No fighting back, son, . . . , no fighting back . . . we can't win that way . . . they'll kill us, baby!" That ill-tempered gorilla would've pulverized my skinny behind if Colonel Washington hadn't held me down. Every now and then, Wash would chuckle and say, "I saved your life, didn't I?"

Years later, when what we had been trying to do became known as the civil rights struggle, I remembered that demeaning experience, and I knew that I wasn't cut out for sitting at lunch counters while being spat on or watching our women being manhandled. As much as I loved and respected Martin Luther King, I guess my role model was more Malcolm X.

I ran into Malcolm a few times back when he was known as "Detroit Red." He was into peddling drugs to musicians, and, although I never got into that life-style, I did chat with him a few times about Omaha. Omaha was his original home, and I had lived there for a while. I didn't see Malcolm again until the sixties. By now, he was a national figure, and all the drug dealing and street life was behind him. During this time, he would summon a group of us to meetings at Richard Morris's house in Los Angeles. Our group usually included Wendell Greene, Don Derricks, and two or three others. Malcolm would appear with four or five Nation of Islam brothers in tow. He didn't proselytize at the get-togethers. His talks to us dealt with standing together, respecting our traditions, defending our communities, treating our women with love and care, being responsible toward our children and not taking abuse from the racists in our society.

The last of these meetings was suddenly different from the others. He had just returned from having completed his pilgrimage to the holy city of Mecca. There were only two Muslim brothers with him this time. There was a feeling of tenseness. As he spoke, his attendants kept moving from the room where we were assembled to the front room where the telephone was located. They seemed to be having trouble getting airline reservations for his return to New York. In none of the earlier meetings had he ever so much as acknowledged that we were old acquaintances.

After his talk, I walked to the end of the room where Mrs. Morris had set out some cookies and punch. I realized that this was the first time I had seen him without a member of his entourage present. As a matter of fact, as he entered the room, the two of us were alone. He quickly stepped across the room and said something like, "Johnny, tell the brothers I'll be back to talk to them soon." In a flash, he was back at the other side of the room. Just as quickly, the attendant came in and whisked him away.

Artistry, Energy, and Fun

*

From my vantage point on the drummer's stool in the Club Alabam, I could see the music that was to be named rhythm and blues taking shape. First in Harlan Leonard's Kansas City Rockets and later, with my own big swing band, the blues and jazz elements were coming together. Neither Harlan's band nor mine could have been described as rhythm and blues, but the acts we were backing at the Alabam in the early and mid-forties were certainly the forerunners of the R&B style. Wynonie Harris, Jo Jo Adams, Marion Abernathy, T-Bone Walker, Little Miss Cornshucks, and Mabel Scott were the kind of artists who headlined the shows. Each of them and the many other blues-oriented performers who starred at the Alabam in those years, had a down-to-earth, uninhibited approach that set them apart from the more formal and formatted jazz and swing performers of the preceding era.

These new show stoppers grew out of the Lionel Hampton, Louis Jordan, Ray Nance, Jimmy Rushing, Illinois Jacquet tradition. The high-spirited exuberance of the African American church tradition and of the little honky-tonk clubs around America was being felt on the stages of the larger, more prestigious Black entertainment rooms. They were demonstrating that artistry, energy, and fun could coexist in Black music without sacrificing artistic integrity. Louis Armstrong had always performed in this way, and now, more and more, the deadpan stiff concept was giving way to a freer, bluesier, more entertaining form. Even in the more conservative world of bebop music, the great Dizzy Gillespie began to use dancing, good humor, and earthiness as a kind of act of love, and his burgeoning popularity among both the music experts and the general public proved him commercially and artistically correct.

As the late Roy Milton once observed, "The trick was to get all that crazy fun we had backstage out to the public." Wynonie Harris had no

With Tom Morgan of Capitol Records and Bardu Ali, band leader and Johnny Otis's partner in the Barrelhouse Club. Morgan and Otis co-produced the recent *Spirit of Black Territory Bands* C.D. album featuring Johnny's present-day band.

trouble with this idea. Some of his song titles, "Who Threw the Whiskey in the Well?," "Don't Roll Those Bloodshot Eyes at Me," and "Good Morning, Judge" are fun even before listening to the records.

Speaking of fun, let vocalist Myra Taylor tell it. "I had just joined Harlan Leonard's band and at our first rehearsal Harlan asked what key I sang Summertime in. I told him B flat. Harlan turned to the band and said, "Okay, fellas, our arrangement is in C, so we'll transpose it to B flat." Trombonist Fred Beckett, who was drunk as a skunk at the time, answered, "Aw right, D flat." Harlan said, "No, B Flat." Beckett blew

Harlan Leonard circa 1940. Leonard learned to play the clarinet at Lincoln High School in Kansas City from Major N. Clark Smith, who also taught Walter Page and Charlie Parker. He joined the Bennie Moten Orchestra in 1923, and in 1931 started his own band, the Kansas City Skyrockets. Leonard later organized the Rockets and recorded with them on Bluebird. Johnny Otis went to L.A. as their drummer in 1943.

spit out of his trombone slide, took a deep breath and said, "Thass what I said, E flat." Saxophonist James Kieth looked back in exasperation and shouted, "B flat, motherfucker! BEE as in Botato!" Almost every old-timer has a story about how they tried to beat going to the army. Red Mack tells of looking through the paper in the early forties and coming across an article about farmers being exempt from military service. "My brother, Joe Morris, owned the Plantation Club out in Watts at that time," Red recalls. "We decided to use the great big parking lot as our farm, so we rented a mule and a plow and worked like mad in the hot sun for two weeks. What did we know about plowing or farming? But we had to establish ourselves as farmers to beat the draft. So, we struggled with that mule, and we finally plowed up that entire huge parking lot. For all the good it did us. The guy at the draft board just looked at me and kept right on inducting me!"

West Oakland

During the thirties and forties and perhaps as far back as the 1920s, there evolved an interesting breed of musicians. They inhabited that musical never-never land that exists somewhere between southern blues and so-called jazz. Usually working for peanuts, in small undistinguished clubs, they made up for whatever technical shortcomings they may have had with enthusiasm and showmanship. They probably regarded themselves as "jazz" players and singers but could be tagged more accurately barrel-house or jump music stylists. A typical jazz musician wouldn't have lasted five minutes in those clubs. The customers weren't interested in musical subtlety or even virtuosity—they wanted spirited entertainment and fun. The bigger the beat, the stronger the boogie woogie flavor, and the bawdier the lyrics, the better.

Of course, bawdy by those standards would hardly raise an eyebrow today. An example of a very daring lyric for that time was the blues Count Otis Matthews sang when we played in those West Oakland greasy spoon dives. It went, "Oohwee, baby, I ain't gonna' do it no more, 'Cause every time I do it, it makes my wee wee sore!" The audience would squeal with delight.

One night in 1941, at the Peavine Club—a tacky Black joint in Reno, Nevada—Count Otis sang his risqué little verse, and a burly, white plainclothes cop materialized out of the shadows and snarled, "Sing one more dirty, filthy song and I'm taking all you niggers down!" After that, our most daring number was "Mama Bought a Chicken."

West Oakland during the thirties and forties was a good example of the contrast between down-home stomp music and sophisticated jazz. At one end of 7th Street was Slim Jenkins' Art Deco club featuring smooth swing/jazz combos, where the audience was well-dressed and

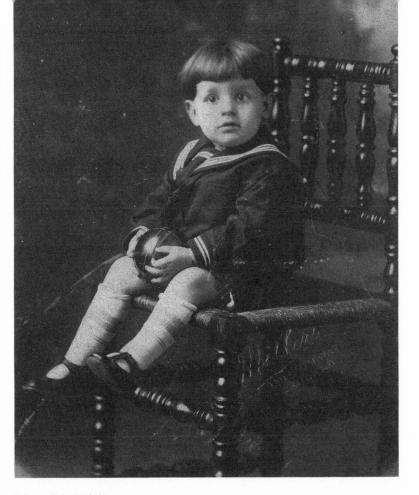

Johnny Otis, Berkeley, 1923.

classy. Farther east on 7th were a number of storefront joints featuring blues and jump bands.

Count Otis, Rudy Jordan, and I would try to slip into Slim's, but we'd usually get thrown out for being too young. When that happened, we would walk up the street to one of the blues joints where we were OK as long as we bought a beer. These places were referred to as Buckets-of-Blood and had a reputation for fights.

The closest thing to a fight I remember was the night two beautiful women came in. Obviously gay, they sat in a booth, sipping their drinks and hugging and kissing. One of them got up and went to the rest room. While she was gone, a half-tipsy dude pulled the other woman out of the booth and tried to force her to dance with him. Returning from the rest room, the other woman tapped the dude on the shoulder and said, "Hey, motherfucker, that's my woman you pullin' on!" He growled, "Fuck you, Bull-Daggin' bitch!" That was a mistake. The lesbian lady grabbed him by the nuts, walked him out the door, and decked him with a right cross. We had many a laugh through the years remembering how he hurried behind her on tiptoe, begging, "Oooh, ooh, please!"

Johnny Otis, Berkeley, California, 1940.

Be-bop, Count Otis Matthews, and Me

At one period in my life, I was so struck by the music of Count Basie, Duke Ellington, and Jimmy Lunceford (especially Basie) that I managed to bury my memories of my days with Count Otis Matthews's West Oakland House Rockers deep in my subconscious. Dazzled by the magic and the glamor of the great swing bands, I purged my thoughts of those styles that, to me, and much of the world, had become "old-fashioned." If I thought of them at all, I thought artists such as George Vann, Louis Armstrong, Tampa Red, Jelly Roll Morton, Robert Johnson, and Bessie Smith were relics of the past. They were, of course, but they were relics from which tradition and the foundations of Black artistry were fashioned. But, back then, try to tell that to me and the army of young musicians who were dead set upon being modern, or even more important, being seen by their peers as modern, because peer pressure had a lot to do with our snobbish attitudes.

I had seen George Vann in West Oakland in 1939 and, at the time, had been moved by his unpretentious pure blues singing and playing. But now, I told myself, that stuff is passé. Louis, Bessie, and all the other "old-timey" blues and jazz artists were best filed away somewhere. I had never seen them anyhow, and as far as Count Otis Matthews was concerned, well, that was just a little jive blues band I had cut my drumming teeth on, no need to embarrass myself in front of the cats by bringing that up.

I proceeded to lose myself in the center of the modern swing music revolution. I played drums on records by Lester Young and Illinois Jacquet. I formed a Basie-style big band, caught a hit record ("Harlem Nocturne"), and traveled all over the country. Prez, Duke, Sweets, Ben Webster, Willie Smith, Earl Warren, Johnny Hodges, Joe Jones, Sonny Greer, James Crawford, Walter Page, Freddy Green, and Jimmy Blanton, these were some of the names that formed my universe. Then, as the forties unfolded, something stunning happened.

Another musical revolution erupted on the African American music scene. Charlie Parker and Dizzy Gillespie presented the jazz world with the higher mathematics of black music—BEBOP! Now, it was the music of Duke, Lunceford, and Basie that was seen as old hat by a new generation of young snobs. I felt very defensive. I thought Basie, Duke, and Lunceford couldn't be invalidated by the emergence of a new musical wrinkle. But bebop was more than a mere wrinkle. It was an all-consuming concept that burned into young musicians like a wild prairie fire. But wasn't this just what had happened with the emergence of the great, straight-ahead swing bands? I came to realize that bebop enthusiasts' scoffing at Duke and Basie was quite the same as what we had done to artists such as Satchmo' and Jelly Roll.

It was time for me to take a long hard look at my flawed perception of artistry and musical evolution. It was time to stop worrying about

Johnny Otis on drums, with Count Otis Matthews and the West Oakland Houserockers, 1940.

what my so-called musically sophisticated friends might think, and to reacquaint myself with the wonderful world of early traditional Black music. Thank God for phonograph records. Even back in the forties, there were 78's on the jazz and blues greats of the twenties and thirties to be found in certain record stores. For the first time in many years, I was bragging and not apologizing about my drumming days with the West Oakland House Rockers.

I used to watch Count Otis empty a whole salt shaker on a bowl of chili mac. "God Damn, man! What are you gonna' do? I KNOW all that salt ain't healthy for you," I'd say. "Shut up, motherfucker!" he'd reply. "Shit. You just don't know what's good!" Count Otis was in his early twenties when he died in the forties. I don't know what he died of, but I suspect loading his bowl of food with salt until it looked like a snow-capped Mount Fuji had something to do with it. By the time I was reevaluating the early styles and feeling good about my time in Count Otis's band, he was gone. How I would've loved to see him and tell him, that in a very special way, my experience with his barrelhouse jump blues band was more valuable to me than even the privilege of playing with Lester Young, Ben Webster, Illinois Jacquet, Lionel Hampton, and Count Basie.

Dropping all the pseudo-elitist notions about what was "best" in music and who was modern and who was dated, helped to prepare me for my role in rhythm and blues.

The Ink Spots Tour

In 1947 I got lucky and landed the coveted Ink Spots Tour. The famous Ink Spots were at the height of their popularity, and every leader of a Black swing band dreamed of being picked to make this lucrative annual trip through the United States and Canada. It meant playing every major city in both countries, all the top theaters and ballrooms, venues we would never have played otherwise.

The 1947 tour consisted of singer June Richmond, comics Willie Lewis and Slappy White (Lewis and White), dancers Honi Coles and Charlie Atkins, my band, and me as emcee for the show, and of course, the world-renowned Ink Spots.

The members of my band (most of us in our twenties) included John Pettigrew, Herb Mullins, and James "Hambone" Robinson on trombones; Art Farmer, Kenneth Medlock, Billy Jones, and Edward Preston, trumpets; Lee Wesley Jones, piano; Junior Raglan, bass; Paul Quinchette and Von Steeter, tenor saxes; William Swindell and Howard Martin, alto saxes; Lem Tally, baritone sax; and Ellis Bartee and myself on drums.

When Bartee left the band, I was urged by some of my players to hire Art Blakey, who was available at the time. My refusal caused a big stir in the band. One by one, the musicians came to me asking that I reconsider. A few of the men, Paul Quinchette, Von Steeter, and Lee Wesley Jones, were close friends, and they gave me hell about it, suggesting that I was reluctant to have Art in the band because he was such a great drummer. He was a great drummer, to be sure, but that wasn't the reason I said no. Finally, out of frustration, I called a meeting to clear up what I knew was a misunderstanding.

I said, "Listen, we're playing mostly theaters, doing four and five shows a day. What is Art Blakey supposed to do while I'm doing my drum solo special every show, sit backstage and twiddle his fingers? While we're at it, why not hire Jo Jones, Max Roach, and Sid Catlett and have them stand by while I do my jive ass solo? It makes me ashamed to think about it."

Ernestine Anderson, sixteen years old at the time, was our female vocalist. June Richmond was the featured singer with the Ink Spots show. She did all the singing when we played theaters, but when we played dance halls or auditoriums, I was able to give Ernestine a solo

New York's Apollo Theatre, 1946.

From right: Alexander Veliotes (Johnny's father), Bardu Ali, Johnny Otis, and Phyllis Otis. On the bar stool opposite Bardu Ali: "Cherry" Otis.

spot. While June Richmond was a dynamic performer, my musicians and I preferred young Ernestine's singing. We could hear those pure jazz and blues elements in her work.

Recently, a friend cracked that finding great women singers was like a holy grail quest with me. As I think about it, that's really true. Starting with Ernestine and including Little Esther Phillips, Etta James, Marie Adams, Sugar Pie Di Santo, Linda Hopkins, Margie Evans, Big Mama Thornton, Barbara Morrison, and up to my current singers, Gail "Little Bit" Muldrow, Ramona and Miss "D," finding and developing gifted female singers has been a special challenge. They begin as raw talent and it's great to see them realize their potential.

It was during the Ink Spots Tour that our first child, Janice, was born.

Eventually, Phyllis and I would have four kids, Janice, Laura, Shuggie, and Nicky.

Going a little farther back in time, I am reminded that our relationship got off to a shaky start. First, the state of California stymied our plans to get married with an ugly, anti-miscegenation law. We were told that we wouldn't have this problem in Nevada, but we came up against the same apartheid mentality in Reno. We got around the problem by having Rudy Jordan go to the city hall with Phyllis and sign my name to the license. Armed with the license, we located a preacher—a white man, there were no Black preachers in Reno in 1941. Instead of delivering the "I now pronounce you" lines, this clown insisted on making racist small talk.

"You people have the God-given gift of singing and dancing, just as we excel in business and government." We had made the mistake of mentioning the fact that I was a musician, and he wouldn't stop complimenting us on our tap-dancing abilities. I came close to telling him where he could shove his little minister's hand book AND the wedding.

The worst was yet to come. Phyllis and I were both underage. Our parents could have the marriage annulled if they chose to. My mother chose to. She sent my father to Reno with specific instructions to break us up legally. But Pop had different ideas.

The first thing he did when he saw Phyllis was to take her in his arms and hug her and kiss her.

"Your mother sent me to annul the marriage, but I came to meet my new daughter," he said in Greek, with tears in his eyes.

"And besides, I don't want to get God on my case."

I never loved that old man more than I did at that moment.

Naughty Lyrics

With the exception of a few blues records with naughty lyrics, most releases in the early days were simply about love or good times. The reason the establishment was so uneasy about the new rhythm and blues discs was the radically new sound. The fact that the musicians and singers were Black didn't help our case either. The straight-laced American moralists saw the new music as alien and subversive.

Not all of those who railed against our music were white, however. Many Black preachers carried on about what they called "the devil's music." Black churchgoers, especially the young, listened to the anti-blues sermons and went out and enjoyed themselves anyhow. They understood that the anti-blues preachers saw the music as competition. If members of the congregation partied with the blues all Saturday night, they probably wouldn't show up in church Sunday morning. They were always preaching against out-of-wedlock sex, too, weren't they? And anybody knew that they would jump over the Empire State Building to get to one of those pretty, big-legged sisters in the choir.

Opposition from certain Black preachers was one thing, but negative actions and attitudes from major record companies, publishing firms, radio and TV stations, ballrooms, and police departments was another—YES, police departments.

The Los Angeles police hounded us in the early days of R&B. They hated to see white kids attending the dances along with Black and Chicano youngsters. As the music grew in popularity, more and more white kids came to our dances, sometimes (God forbid!), even dancing with African American and Mexican American teenagers. At first, the cops would stand around glaring at the kids and harassing them with bullshit questions, checking their ID's, and so on. This was damaging enough, but eventually they began to use ancient blue laws against us. These old laws read as follows: it is unlawful for a fifteen-year-old to dance with a sixteen-year-old, a sixteen-year-old shall not dance with a seventeen-year-old, a seventeen-year-old must not dance with an eighteen-year-old, and so forth. These tactics completely disrupted our dances, and we were unable to continue promoting dances in the Los Angeles area.

Finally we moved our Saturday night R&B dances to the American Legion Stadium in El Monte, a small town near Los Angeles. Eventually, though, the El Monte city fathers revoked our dance license. Racism, under the guise of all-American morality, had triumphed again.

It's really interesting how a little money can override concerns about racial purity and morality. When we paid off the firemen and police, as we often did in Long Beach and other Southern California cities, we had no more trouble. Just like back in the good old days of bootleg liquor, only we weren't handling an illegal product.

They say music hath charm to soothe the savage breast. That may be true in some instances, but our music enraged the racists and pious moralists. In the mid-fifties, KFOX radio station manager, Hal Sheidler, hired me to do a daily disc jockey show. That same day, he introduced me to the owner, a Texas oil man named Fetch. The first words out of Fetch's mouth were, "Don't you play none of that goddamned nigger music!" He was livid with rage at the thought, and we hadn't even said hello yet. Sheidler gave me a "be cool" sign behind Fetch's back, and as Fetch sold the station a short time later, it didn't matter. I was now a disc jockey playing my rhythm and blues records.

By 1955, I had a television show in addition to the radio show. The TV show was a weekly, half-hour live musical featuring the people in my band and special guest artists. Every week was a different guest star, usually artists we were promoting somewhere in Southern California: Ray Charles, the Coasters, Sam Cooke, Ike and Tina Turner, The Drifters, and so on. Our regulars included Marie Adams and the Three Tons of Joy, Little Arthur Matthews, Mel Williams, Julie Stephens, Trudy Williams, Kansas City Bell, Don Johnson, George Washington, Jimmy Nolan, Jackie Kelso, Fred Harmon, and Johnny Parker.

With my radio and television shows we were able to present popular attractions throughout Southern California. At one point, we had Chuck Berry booked to appear at the Long Beach Municipal Auditorium. My partner in these endeavors, Hal Zeiger, assured me he had greased the cops, so there shouldn't be any problems. But certain church and parent groups had begun making noises about the negative effects of R&B music on the young. We were informed that they would be sending a large committee to monitor the affair. I knew where the group was seated, and during the dance, I kept an anxious eye on them hoping they would approve. We almost never had fights or disturbances at dances, but with 3,000 or 4,000 exuberant kids, we just prayed that everything would go smoothly.

I brought Chuck Berry on, and the crowd cheered. I glanced up in the balcony where the protectors of teenage morality were seated, and they seemed to be smiling. Then Chuck Berry blasted forth with:

> We did it in the kitchen . . .
> We did it in the hall . . .
> I got some on my finger . . .
> And I wiped it on the wall.

The kids squealed with delight. Holy shit! Our goose was surely cooked! But there was so much background noise in the auditorium that the members of the committee didn't seem to catch the lyrics.

In the past, we have received a lot of flack on two songs I wrote, namely, "Dance with Me Henry" and "Willie and the Hand Jive." Sometimes the record companies would get edgy about song titles and change them. When Etta James and I wrote "Roll With Me Henry," it was a dance record. This song, which became Etta's first hit, was changed from "Roll with Me Henry" to "The Wallflower." Finally, Georgia Gibbs's sanitized version, retitled "Dance with Me Henry," prevailed. The furor finally subsided, but not before they ran us through three different song titles and a lot of silly and unnecessary changes.

In the case of my song "Willie and the Hand Jive," the morbid titillation continues to this day. Last year, during a National Public Radio show, the interviewer asked on the air, "Is 'Hand Jive' really about masturbation?" I was surprised. This, from a broadcast agency known for its maturity and common sense. In my frustration, I almost blurted out, "Damn! can't you hear the lyrics? It's about dancing . . . DANCING!"

In 1970 Delmar "Mighty Mouth" Evans, my son Shuggie, and I put together an album of obscene and bawdy ballads: stuff that had been around a long time. Some of it, I've been told by musicologists, has been sung since the turn of the century, but never publicly. We used rhythm and blues rhythms. These were very naughty poems and ditties that Delmar and I had heard through the years in pool halls, in jails, and in the streets. "The Signifyin' Monkey" had been done before but always scrubbed clean of the original lyrics. We decided to present the songs in unexpurgated form with all the original shocking expletives intact. In addition to "The Signifyin' Monkey," we did "The Pissed-Off Cowboy," "Hey Shine," "Cream Dream," and "The Great Stack-a-Lee."

We titled the album, Snatch and the Poontangs. I added a large FOR ADULTS ONLY on the cover to help to reduce the chance of being hassled. We were learning more and more as time went by, that our First Amendment rights were apt to be trampled by the self-righteous and self-appointed keepers of American morals.

Delmar and I wanted to preserve these old bawdy songs on record, just as the British preserve their limerick tradition. Of course, the English have a broader national sense of humor than we do. Laughing about sex or bodily functions may be in bad taste, according to one's perspective, but in England, I never found it to be grounds on which to throw someone in jail. Knowing that our butts could land in jail because of the album, I decided not to mention our names anywhere on it. I became Snatch, Delmar was Mighty Mouth, and Shuggie's alias was Prince Wunnerful.

This album didn't start out as an effort to preserve ancient compositions for posterity. At first, we were just having fun in my backyard studio. After a while, as we played them back, we realized, hey, this stuff

Rock and Roll Fan Club, Jordan High School, Watts, 1957.

would probably sell. To this day, we have never had a hint of a threat of censorship or legal action on this very raw record. "Hand Jive" and "Roll with Me, Henry," two perfectly clean records, on the other hand, have stirred up a lot of controversy through the years. But then, Snatch and the Poontangs was never a big hit either.

Jailhouse Blues

In the late sixties, we were booked into a seedy Vegas night club for a ten-day run. We made the trip from L.A. on a sunny, summer day. Fourteen of us, plus a couple of our girl singer's children were on our old bus, Nellie Belle. Nellie Belle Five, actually, as this was my fifth band bus through the years. I bought Nellie Belle from Ray Charles. She had seen her best days, but I kept the engine tuned-up tight, and she was very dependable on the highway.

Our spirits were high. This was going to be kind of a vacation gig. Not a lot of money, but we were told that the hotel we would stay in was nice enough, with a swimming pool and a playground for the kids. All this was true, except for the money part. I was promised five grand for the gig, payable $500 per night. As it turned out, I got no hundred dollars per night.

I went to the club owner at the end of the first night, and he informed me the agent was the one who pays and that I should contact him. This had not been my understanding. I went immediately to the phone and called the man I had made the deal with.

I told the agent, "The club owner says you're the money man on this gig, and I'm looking for the $500 a night you promised me."

"Don't worry about it, I'll take care of it in the morning," he assured me.

A little warning bell went off inside my head. As a result of some bad experiences early in my career, I made it a rule to never go on a job without a security deposit of at least 50 percent. In this case, while I had never actually done business with the agent, I'd known him for a long time. This engagement had come up at the last minute, and I didn't feel I had to worry about a deposit.

I couldn't catch up with him the next day. I called the group together,

(Left) Johnny Otis and B. B. King in Houston, 1950. Starting in 1951, King would go on to have more than 70 best-selling rhythm and blues records. (Right) Johnny Otis and B. B. King in Compton, California, 1986.

and we decided to play one more night and hope for the best. Just before showtime, I caught up with the agent by phone, and he gave me his word he'd meet me at the club after the last show with the money. He didn't show, and now I was really worried.

I finally got him on the phone again the following morning. "I'll be there at noon with the money," he assured me, "And what are you worried about? You've got my P.A. system as collateral. If you don't get paid, the sound system is yours."

He didn't show by noon. At two o'clock we decided to give it up and go home. By three o'clock, we were packed and heading for L.A.—kids, equipment, performers, P.A. system, and all.

"Don't worry, Hawk," the Mighty Flea shouted from the back of the bus, "That's a pretty good sound system. We'll probably get a couple hundred bucks for it at the pawn shop."

Ordinarily, on the way home from a gig, we'd be in a good mood, happy to be on the way back home. This trip we were broke and disgusted. The usually good-natured Three Tons of Joy were very quiet. The young Otisettes were trying to calm the kids who were disappointed at having to leave so soon. Every person on the bus was depressed, all silently trying to figure out how to get around this financial disaster. At home, rents would be due, bills piling up. I was thankful that the whole gang didn't come down on me for botching up the business. They mercifully let me slide. But not for long.

Delmar Evans started it. "Hey, what the hell happened to your iron-clad rule of never going on a gig without a deposit?"

"Well, I blew it this time" I muttered. "I've known this dude for a long time, y'know . . . and I was thinking. . . ."

"Well, while you was thinking, what made you think that low-class, white motherfucker would hesitate to screw us?!!"

This set off an avalanche of recriminations. Nothing much I could say in defense because I had goofed. Finally the noise quieted down. Millie Calhoun, one of the Three Tons, sat down beside me and said, "Don't feel bad, John, you made a mistake, but we all know you didn't want this to happen."

"I said, "Thanks, baby."

The day we got home, the L.A. police picked me up and took me to jail. The agent had me arrested, claiming I stole his P.A. system and moved it across a state line. I had been in jail twice before. The first time on a draft-dodging charge. My induction notice had been sent to a pre-

With "The Three Tons of Joy," Marie Adams, Francielle McKinny, and Doris McKinny in Los Angeles, 1957.

vious address, and my former landlady had failed to forward the papers, which resulted in me being listed as a draft dodger. I spent eight days in jail before being cleared.

The second time I was arrested, it was for asking a cop to loosen the handcuffs on a youngster who had attended a record hop I hosted at South Park in L.A. The kid was screaming in pain. The cuffs had been put on sideways and were causing him a lot of pain. Ten seconds after I asked the cop to ease the boy's misery, they slapped cuffs on me and arrested me for interfering with police business. Now I knew why the kid was crying. My cuffs were on sideways, too.

I know that jails are not designed to be pleasant vacation resorts, but I was totally unprepared for what I saw and lived through for three days after being arrested.

The first thing that struck me was the fact that almost all the prisoners I saw—and I saw hundreds—were Black or Mexican. Anyone seeing this and not knowing any better, would assume that whites did not commit crimes, that only African Americans and Mexicans were wrongdoers. There were very, very few whites.

I always thought that men and women were kept completely separate in jails. While we weren't housed together in cells or holding tanks, we were brought into close contact more than once. The way we were brought together was degrading.

A line of us were being marched down a corridor when a group of women appeared, coming in the opposite direction. As we lined up next to one another, we were ordered to halt and the cops made cracks like: "Hey! Pussy, fifty cents a feel, ass a quarter!" The women stood with their heads hung down. The men were quiet. The cops were guffawing, and I never felt more dehumanized in my life.

Later, about a hundred of us were put into a large glass room and told to strip. When we were naked, large doors across the aisle were thrown open. Inside, women were dressing. The cops thought this was hilarious.

One very young Chicano kid was terrified by the experience. He appeared to be constantly smiling, but this was his facial expression. A cop told him, "Wipe that fuckin' smile off your face!" When the kid couldn't do it, the cop slapped him so hard, blood flew everywhere.

At one point, several hundred of us were packed into a room with a few phones on the wall. Because of the short time we were allowed and the crush, not many of us got to make a call. As I waited to make a call (which I never got to do) I heard a Black youngster say into the phone, "I don't know, mama. I didn't do nothing . . . please get me out!" His mama probably had as much chance of coming up with money for a $500 bond (maybe more) as a snowball in hell.

I hope I never have an experience like that again, but I thank God that I did. I know that men and women are packed into the jails right now, this minute, and are being treated like dogs. I saw many hundreds of prisoners during that experience. There is no way I can be sure which were innocent and which were guilty. One thing I do know however, is that I saw criminal police. I also know that no human being, innocent or guilty, should be treated the way we were.

PART 3

THE MUSICIANS

Prez: Lester Young

Why does Lester Young rate a chapter in a book about rhythm and blues? Because, like a hungry, prowling fox, from the thirties up to the present time, he left tracks everywhere—no matter how faint. Even if a blues or jazz musician claims Coleman Hawkins or Ben Webster as his or her primary influence, the fact remains that Prez is always lurking in the background, and in the case of most players, Lester is sitting right down front. Charlie Parker, Willis Jackson, King Curtis, Dexter Gordon, Lee Allen, Illinois Jacquet, Plas Johnson, and dozens—actually, hundreds—of other sax players recite the gospel of Lester Young with every other breath they blow.

I am a Lester Young fanatic, to put it mildly, but I am just one of many. Within our ranks are the Prez aficionados who feel personally abused when their hero is attacked. Preston Love is one of these. Once, in Count Basie's band (after Lester had gone), tenor sax Lucky Thompson threw a verbal tantrum because one of the players referred to Lester in a laudatory and nostalgic manner. Thompson railed about "that bullshit that Lester Young played." It took three of the Basie men to pull an enraged Preston Love aside and cool him off. And a good thing, too, because Love, a former Midwest, Golden Gloves heavyweight champion might have ended Thompson's sax blowing career right then and there with a sledge hammer right to the chops! The fact is, that Thompson, with all his professed disdain for Lester Young, was to some degree, just like all the others, under the magic spell of Lester. And all the better for it, too, I might add.

Nor did Lester stamp his brand on sax players alone. B. B. King is quick to name Prez a melodic role model. Little Esther Phillips, as a young girl, used to tell me how much she idolized Dinah Washington. This was, of course, quite obvious, but once she added, "Hey, Lester

Johnny Otis and Don Robey in Houston, Texas, circa 1952. Photo by Ernest C. Withers, copyright 1993, Mimosa Records Prod., Inc.

Young gets in my head all the time." Billie Holiday's worship of Lester's artistry is legendary. There's no mistaking his strong presence in her singing.

Back in the forties, Lester overheard one of my friends call me "Hawk" (as in hawk nose). From that moment on, I was Lady Hawk to him. Nothing negative intended: he called everybody lady something or other. Some years later, as I was getting off the elevator at the Chicago Pershing Hotel, I heard him call out, "Hey Lady Hawk, let me see your machine-o'reenie." Don Robey had just bought me a new portable tape recorder to help me as I scouted talent for his Peacock record label.

Even the most portable models weighed a ton in those days, so, I was happy to stop by his room. I would've been delighted anyhow, of course, because to spend time with Prez was to enjoy his "o'reenie, o'roonie" language and to just bask in the glow of his gentle genius.

Musicians and entertainers were automatically assigned rooms on the fourth floor of the Pershing Hotel. If a blind man got off on the fourth floor, he would know immediately where he was, because the atmosphere was always thick with the aroma of pot:

VON STEETER: "Have a little a little little hit, J.O."
ME: "Man, you know I don't smoke that stuff."
VON STEETER: "You might as well, you live on the fourth floor—you gonna' get contact high anyhow . . . ha, ha!"

I'd give my right arm to have the tape Lester and I made that afternoon. Somehow, through the years, it got away from me. Maybe somebody lifted it? I don't know. I wish I had it now so I could transcribe it verbatim. But I've relived it so many times in my mind that I remember a lot of what we chatted about.

LESTER: "So, the Little Esthereenie kittie was a good lick o'reenie for you, huh?"
J.O.: "Yeah, the little chick was a blessing for us. She's raisin' sand all over the country."
LESTER: "Y'all eatin' regular now . . . dig." [chuckle]
J.O.: "Yeah, and payin' the rent too, sometimes."
LESTER: "They'll be tryin' to copy her song, evonce—that's the stuff you gotta' watch, dig."

"EVONCE" was another Lester Young secret punctuation word that nobody knew the actual meaning of.

As a kid, Lester was playing in the Young family band. Often this meant minstrel-type performances in the Deep South. The shows featured high-energy showmanship, often in demeaning blackface makeup and outrageous circus costumes. Lester's nephew Jimmy Tolbert explains that young Prez refused to indulge in Big Jay McNeely-style rolling-on-the-floor antics. As the various family members were jumping over each other's backs, doing splits and wildly carrying on all over the stage, Lester's idea of flash was to hold his horn sideways and up high, a habit that stayed with him throughout his career.

I remember we had to put on funny hats to amuse the white folks during my time with George Morrison's band in Denver, but that was the early forties, and blackface makeup and overt Uncle Tomming was not something we had to do in Denver during that time. The cutesy hats were degrading enough, however. The older musicians used to tell us about the twenties and thirties when earning a living in the lesser

Prez Lester Young (1909–1959).

territory bands hinged on one's willingness to swallow pride and act the buffoon.

The white-territory bands didn't experience the same degree of humiliation. They were required to don funny hats and clown at times, but it was not racially degrading, as it was in our case. Moving from town to town in our little raggedy school buses, having to go to the back door of restaurants to get something to eat, and being turned away at flea bag hotels and having to sleep in the freezing or sweltering bus—all this was hard to take. But the biggest hardship was the funny hats and having to suffer through some of our bandleader's Uncle Tommish renditions such as "Sonny Boy" or "Shine." George Morrison was a lovely person, but he would whip out his violin at a moment's notion, sit on a stool center-stage, and do a version of "Shine" that would fill the musicians with shame and anger. The white folks loved it, of course, but this only made matters worse. George Morrison rejected the idea that this was kissin' white folk's asses. He referred to it as "Black Diplomacy" and pointed out that without the "Sonny Boy" and "Shine" features, we wouldn't be working. Of course, he had a point.

Young Family Band, with Lester Young. One of the great innovators on the tenor saxophone, Young refused to tour in the South with the Young Family Band, quit, and took up the saxophone in the 1920s. He played with the Blue Devils, the Bennie Moten Orchestra, and briefly with Fletcher Henderson. He made tremendously important records with Basie in the 1930s, had three rhythm and blues hits on the Keynote label in 1944, and recorded for the Los Angeles Aladdin label between 1945 and 1948.

Lester came up in the twenties and thirties when experiencing what we had to bear in the forties and fifties would've been considered mild. In spite of what he went through, however, I don't hear hardship in Lester's playing. I hear a melancholy power and a lament, but I also hear a joyous celebration of life, the human spirit, and sexuality. But then, I'm a Lester Young freak. To me, Prez is the one figure who stands above the entire field of music as the guiding spirit of African American artistry.

Sweets Edison remembers that Prez "could play anything he thought of." Anyone who plays an instrument and does any improvising, knows that, like reading music, you must be a few bars ahead of yourself at all times. Your brain says, "I'm coming up to the so-and-so part, so I'll play thus and so." But we also have a little monitor sitting up there—I certainly do, because of my technical limitations—and this monitor might tell us, "Yeah, that's a great idea, but don't try it!" So, you either modify the idea or go on to safer ground.

Lester didn't have that problem. He heard something in his head and he played it. In addition, Lester almost never indulged in reference ditties during a solo. You won't suddenly hear "Yankee Doodle Went to Town" in the middle of a Lester Young solo. He's usually too busy telling marvelous original stories to be bothered with frivolity.

Count Basie

The year was 1945. I was returning some arrangements Count Basie had allowed me to copy and put into my band book. It was Chicago and Basie was staying in a small hotel on South Parkway.

"Hi, Base."

"Hi, John."

"Here are the manuscripts you loaned me, and I wanna thank you, too."

"Oh, okay, just put 'em right here on that chair. Sit down and have some ribs. . . . The fight'll be on the radio in a minute."

"Hey, thanks, don't mind if I do. Damn, Base! You got enough ribs to feed half the South Side!"

Two of the largest slabs of barbecue I'd ever seen in my life were laid out on his lap in the bed. The fight broadcast began as we chomped away. Joe Louis was fighting someone, and it's been so many years ago, I've forgotten who his opponent was. I ducked out to get us some soda pop, and as I came back, Basie was sitting straight up in the bed. The action had heated up and the announcer was excited. In between bites of barbecue, Basie was shouting, "Get him, Joe! . . . Get him, baby!" This was before everyone had television sets. Then, radio broadcasts were our only link to the fights and baseball games. As the action wound up, all three of us were hollering—the announcer, Basie, and I.

It is quite impossible to explain to today's generation just what Joe Louis meant to us back in those days. He was our special hero, our personal sense of self-worth, our pride and joy, OUR BLACK SUPERMAN. White society kicked our asses every day, but when Joe Louis won a fight, our hearts soared. All over this weary, Jim Crow land, Black folk had to sit in the back of the bus, but when Joe flattened a white fighter we stood ten feet tall. The American deck was stacked against our people, but when the Brown Bomber struck, we felt we had won a hand. "Get him, Joe! Get that motherfucker, baby!"

Suddenly, Joe shot one of those devastating, lightning fast jabs, and the announcer screamed, "He's down! . . . He's down! . . . He's flat on his back! . . . I don't think he can survive that vicious shot to the head. . . . I think it's all over, folks!" Unlike TV, where you can plainly see what's happening, radio broadcasts could be nerve-wracking. With a mouth full of barbecue, Basie was shouting, "Who's down? . . . Who's down, goddammit?!!"

"The Brown Bomber chalks up another victory!" the announcer added. Damn! That was a relief! It wasn't Joe down on his back, after all. I turned to say something to Basie, and I saw that his eyes were

Johnny Otis, Count Basie, and Nicky Otis, 1981 or 1982. Born in Red Bank, New Jersey, Basie (1904–1984) played piano and organ. He joined a group fronted by Walter Page in 1928, then played with the Bennie Moten Orchestra before starting his own orchestra. He had one of the most famous and most respected swing bands of all time for such numbers as "One O'Clock Jump," "Sent for You Yesterday, Here You Come Today," "Good Morning Blues," "Taxi War Dance," and "Lester Leaps In." Basie's group also had novelty R&B flavored hits in the 1940s with "Rusty Dusty Blues," "Red Bank Boogie," "Jimmy's Blues," and "Open the Door Richard."

bulging and he was gagging. In the heat of the moment, he had choked on a piece of barbecue. I ran over and pounded him on the back. We didn't know about any Heimlich maneuver back then. He coughed up the piece of meat and with tears in his eyes, laid back on the pillow, and gasped for breath.

When he had regained his composure, I said, "Just in case you were planning to charge me for those arrangements, I don't owe you shit, 'cause I just saved your life."

"Yeah," he replied. "But you ate $20 worth of my ribs!"

The last time I saw count Basie was a few years ago at Harrah's Casino in Lake Tahoe. It was just prior to his death. He was performing in the main room, and my band and I were in the lounge. It broke my heart to see him in a wheelchair. My larger-than-life idol couldn't get old and sick! But no matter how I hated the thought, though, there he was, winding down.

"The wheelchair's a drag, Johnny, but it beats the hell out of not being here at all," he said philosophically. We talked about the old days and how, just a few years back, Black people couldn't come into the casinos in Tahoe, Reno, or Las Vegas, at all, let alone work as featured performers. We concluded that African Americans, on the whole, still got the short end of the stick but that some things had changed for the better.

I told him, "I think the way for Black folks to beat the system in America is to play piano or basketball." Basie was not one to do much talking about politics or the social situation, so, the little bitter chuckle he gave me was a lot for him. But for one to assume that he didn't harbor deep resentment over the way his people were mistreated in this country would be a mistake. I always found him a bit reserved and removed about everything. His display of emotion as we listened to the Joe Louis fight was a glimpse of the passion that lay just below the surface, but it was very uncharacteristic of him as a rule. As a matter of fact, this is how he usually functioned at the piano—understated and subtle, but given to occasional flashes of musical thunder. His was a well-modulated style of plinks and planks that usually concealed the deep reservoir of heat that lurked just below the surface.

Count Basie was not known for civil rights speeches or emotional outbursts, but he had his moments—at times he could raise hell about racism. Preston Love, who played lead alto sax with Basie for a number of years, remembers a time in 1945 when "it was the policy of the Southern California Meadowbrook to shunt Black customers to the dim recesses at the rear of the hall. Basie was complaining about this practice

From left: Jo Jones, Preston Love, and Michael Silva, Paris, 1983. Jo Jones (1911–1985) played drums for the Count Basie Orchestra, where he was responsible for the beats that made the band famous. His tendency to minimize the bass drum, to keep time with top cymbal, and to use the rest of the drums for embellishments had an enormous influence on Max Roach, Kenny Clarke, and other Be-Bop Era drummers.

one evening, and the ballroom manager disdainfully flipped a book of matches at him and told him to 'Calm down, take it easy!' That set Basie off. He slammed the guy against the wall and told him where he could shove the Meadowbrook Ballroom. 'You stop sticking my people in the back of the hall, or I'm taking my band outta here!'"

In that same year, at the Queensway Ballroom in Toronto, Canada, an announcer stepped to the mike in his tuxedo just before the band was to start playing and said, "Ladies and gentlemen, the Queensway Ballroom presents the Count of swing and jive, so, have a wonderful time, . . . blah, blah, blah, but remember there is to be no mixed dancing." Basie got up from the piano and stepped back stage. The band could hear him roaring to Henry Snodgrass, the chief roadie, "Pack up! Let's get out of this motherfucker!" The guy who had delivered the apartheid announcement sheepishly stepped back to the microphone and muttered, "Please ignore my previous announcement about mixed dancing."

Preston further recalls a day, circa 1946, when he and Jimmy Rushing were checking into a Philadelphia hotel. The lady at the desk had her radio on, and coincidentally, Basie was being interviewed over a local radio station concerning their upcoming Earle Theatre engagement. "Well, Count," the interviewer said, "So, you and the band are back in town . . . tell me, is that boy Jimmy Rushing still with the band?" Big pause. Finally, Basie said icily, "First of all, Jimmy Rushing is not a boy . . . he's a man and a great blues singer, and yes, he is still with the band."

In 1944, Phyllis and I were living in a dingy hotel on Washington Boulevard in L.A. My Central Avenue gig with Harlan Leonard had played out. I was out of a job and broke. This was before I became the house bandleader at the Club Alabam. My friends, Sonny Love (Preston's brother), Bob Reid, and our soon-to-be, first Black basketball star, Don Barksdale, lived in the same building. We all pooled our pennies, and Phyllis kept us alive with spaghetti and Kool Aid. One early evening, someone shouted, "Hey, Johnny Otis, you're wanted on the phone." I ran down the hall to the public pay phone. God! I hope this is a gig!

The voice on the other end of the line said, "Hello Johnny, this is Earl Fatha Hines. Listen, Shadow Wilson has come down sick and had to go back to New York. Can you bring your drums down to the Plantation Club and finish the week with us?" My heart jumped! A gig with a big name band! I said, "Yessir, Mr. Hines!" (Hallelujah! to myself!) "By the way," he continued, "The job is yours permanently if you want it. I can only offer you $150 a week at first, but you'll get more when we play the Apollo Theatre."

"Yessir, YESSIR, Mr. Hines!" SHEEEEIT! A hundred and fifty dollars a week! That was a small fortune back in 1944. I think my dad was making $35 or $40 a week at the time, working at the Mare Island Navy Yard in Vallejo. New York! The Apollo Theatre! ALLRIGHT!"

"I'm glad you double on oboe. That's important because we have a couple of oboe features for you."

"Oboe?"

"Yes, Oboe."

"Man, I don't play no oboe."

"What? You can't play oboe? Well, we can't use you then because your drumming ain't that strong by itself."

My heart sank. This had to be a cruel joke.

"Who is this," I demanded.

"This is Earl Fatha Hines, I told you."

"You're fulla' shit!"

"Oh yeah, well fuck you, nigger! You can't play oboe, you can't have the job."

Suddenly, I recognized the voice. "Ellis Bartee, you little silly bastard! I'm gonna' kill you for this!"

Two weeks later, once again, "Johnny Otis, telephone."

"Hello."

"Hello, Johnny Otis. This is Bill Basie. Jo Jones is sick, can you come out to the Plantation Club and finish the engagement with us?"

"You little, jive-ass, stupid motherfucker" I barked, "Do you really think you're gonna' catch me on that same shit twice?!"

"Gasp . . . Ahem . . ."

Guess what? It was really Basie! We laughed about that many times through the years.

Ellis Bartee was the Kansas City drummer who had played in Hamp's big band and later in mine. He was a fine drummer but an incorrigible prankster. He haunted the novelty shops in search of some gimmick with which to play jokes on someone—a lifelike rubber snake or tarantula spider, itching powder, a hand buzzer. One evening he slipped a whoopee cushion into the chair of a very sophisticated society matron during a backstage reception. When she sat down everyone thought she had blasted off the most humongous fart in history. How terribly embarrassing for the poor lady, but funny as hell.

When I told Basie why I had thought his phone call was a sham, and how Bartee had put the hoax on me the week before, he laughed and said, "I know that little sucker from Kansas City, and I'm not surprised."

T-Bone Walker

There were many great musicians living in various cities during the early days of rhythm and blues development who never performed on a record and therefore, had no national reputation and exerted little, if any, influence on the final product. Among the piano players whose styles were well-known by virtue of their recordings and who helped shape the early R&B sounds were Charles Brown, Jay McShann, Count Basie, Pete Johnson, Meade Lux Lewis, Avery Parrish, and Albert Ammons. Some of the great women boogie and blues players were Cleo Brown, Julia Lee, Camille Howard, Nellie Lutcher, Mary Lou Williams, and Hazel Scott. The early saxophone influences were Louis Jordan, Ben Webster, Eddie Vinson, Illinois Jacquet, Arnett Cobb, Buddy Floyd, and Lester Young. A bit later came Clifford Scott, Earl Bostic, Lee Allen, Plas Johnson, and King Curtis. There were other important players on both piano and saxophone, of course, but the above readily come to mind.

Where rhythm and blues guitar is concerned, there is no need to strain the memory to come up with who the original influences were. There was exactly one. T-Bone. Aaron Thibeaux Walker. He single-handedly defined what rhythm and blues guitar was all about. From him spring B. B. King, Pee Wee Crayton, Freddy King, Albert Collins, Albert King, Buddy Guy, Lowell Fulson, Pete Lewis, Gatemouth Brown, Chuck Berry, and all the others down to the present day, who fall under the category of rhythm and blues guitarist. There was, however, one man, who brought an original, delicate, jazz-tinged touch to Rhythm and Blues. His name was Johnny Moore, but he too borrowed heavily from the old master.

T-Bone, as his records attest, was more than an instrumentalist. He was also a blues and blues ballad singer supreme. On stage he exhibited another strength. He was a marvelous showman. In the days before

Born in Texas, T-Bone Walker (1910–1975) worked as "lead boy" for Blind Lemon Jefferson on Central Avenue in Dallas in the 1920s. He won a talent contest sponsored by Cab Calloway and toured with the Calloway and Milt Larkin bands before moving to Los Angeles in 1934. There he worked at the Little Harlem Club. Generally acknowledged as the founder of the blues electric guitar style, Walker had nine Top Twenty rhythm and blues hit records between 1947 and 1950. Photos courtesy of Michael Ochs Archives.

electronic remote devices, T-Bone would use a long extension cord from his guitar to his amplifier that enabled him to wander far into the audience when he played. My band and I appeared along with T-Bone at a Cavalcade of Jazz concert at Wrigley Field in Los Angeles during the mid-forties. It was the first time the musicians in my band and I had seen him use the long extension cord. It blew us and the crowd away. At first, we could hear him strumming one of his bluesy introductions, but he was nowhere to be seen. At the sound of his guitar, the crowd went wild. They knew it was T-Bone. But where was he? Suddenly, he came struttin' out of the side of the ballpark. Across the field he strode and into the crowd. Before he got to the main body of the audience, he had a bevy of young women touching him, kissing, and hugging him.

He was just as dynamic when he played in a club. We had T-Bone as the star attraction when I was the leader of the house band at the Club Alabam. In clubs, however, there was more than mere hugging and kissing from the ladies. By the time he got to his flash finale where he would raise the guitar over his shoulders and fall into a slow split, the floor was covered with panties and money. The chicks didn't snatch their drawers off and throw them. They brought extras in their purses. I know, 'cause I was watching like a hawk.

T-Bone was handsome, charismatic, super talented, and at the same time sweet and unassuming. In addition to all that good stuff, he brought us a brilliant guitar style that helped form the basis for rhythm and blues and rock and roll.

Mister Blues: Wynonie Harris

During the heyday of R&B, we seldom did concerts, and festival gigs were unknown at the time. Night clubs, auditoriums, even tobacco warehouses were the order of the day. There existed extended engagements at large hotels but not for us—only white bands got those. For the most part, it was a life of one-nighters. During my territory band days, I remember doing eight or ten one-nighters in a row. With the Lloyd Hunter band it was high school auditoriums, jitney (Dime-a-Dance) halls, farm buildings, and an occasional amusement park job such as Peony Park in Omaha. There were Black theaters in the east and down south featuring musical stage shows, but in order to get those bookings a group had to first attain name band status. Once we scored a hit record, the entire country became our territory. Fifty or sixty one-nighters in a row was not unusual.

If I announced, "We're going to the Apollo!" it would set off a celebration in the band bus. Whenever we played the Apollo, we also played a string of other theaters. This theater circuit was known as "Around the World." Around the World included The Royal Theatre in Baltimore, the Howard in Washington, D.C., The Paradise in Detroit, the Regal in Chicago, the Earle in Philadelphia, and of course, the famous Apollo in Harlem.

These were week-long engagements. They ran from openings on Friday to closings on Thursday. Shows would start in the mornings and wind up in the evenings. When we were red hot, coming off a hit record, the crowds were so thick we would do six, even seven shows a day. Hard work, but it beat the one-nighter grind in many important ways. In the East, where these theaters were located, we had no trouble finding a restaurant that would serve us or a hotel to stay in. We lived within the African American communities, and as a result, were not subject to the same kinds of racist pressures that we encountered elsewhere, especially in the Deep South.

On the bill with us in these theaters would appear many wonderful performers of the era. The Peters Sisters, Peg Leg Bates, Pigmeat Markham, Moms Mabley, the Four Step Brothers, Bunny Briggs, John "Spider Bruce" Mason, the High Hatters, Little Miss Cornshucks, Marion Abernathy, Wynonie Harris, Little Miss Sharecropper who later would gain stardom as Laverne Baker, and Redd Foxx and Slappy White, known professionally in those days as Foxx and White.

Playing the Black theaters of the big cities in the East was a treat and a relief. For a while, at least, no more unloading, checking into hotels, repacking, checking out, and moving on to the next city on the one-nighter itinerary. At that pace, we hardly had a chance to catch our breath, let alone meet someone and relax. Oh, but during the theater dates we could meet beautiful girls and spend time together! Being in the music world and working to enhance your career and reputation was a strong incentive to go on the road. Making a living was an important factor, too, of course. But swimming in a sea of adoring beautiful women was heaven on earth. To describe the romantic thrills of the classic rhythm and blues era culture may be considered politically incorrect by certain of today's notions, but it seems to me, that the truth is always worth dealing with: and the plain truth is, being popular and being on stage brought the young men and women in the bands unlimited opportunities to meet and be with attractive members of the opposite sex, or the same sex, for that matter, if that happened to be your persuasion.

Recently, an interviewer asked me if I would trade my memories of the old days for anything. I said, "Be real." Then, he asked, "The music, the pretty women, the touring, the good times, would you do it all over again?" All I could think of as an answer, was what Muhammed Ali once asked of Howard Cosell, "IS YOU A FOOL?"

A cardinal rule of those early days was, never allow Wynonie Harris to get anywhere near you if you were in the company of a young lady. He had a warped sense of humor that bordered on devilish cruelty. If he managed to sneak up on you while you were walking with your girl friend or sitting with her in a restaurant or club, you were in trouble.

"Excuse me, young lady, I don't mean no harm, but this low-down motherfucker is married to my sister, and I don't appreciate what's going on here!"

"Gasp!"

"Don't pay him no mind, baby. He just likes to kid a lot. Cut it out, Wynonie!"

Preston Love working as musical director for Motown in 1968. He is shown here with Aretha Franklin.

"Kidding, my ass, you adulterer. You know I'm telling the truth."

"Wynonie, get outa' here with that mess. This girl knows you're fulla shit!"

But the girl is affected by what Wynonie is saying. You can see it in her eyes.

"I told my sister not to marry you, you dog! Now, here you are deceiving this innocent girl, knowing damn well that your wife will be arriving here at any time!"

"I'll see you later," the young woman snaps and hurries off.

By the time you turn to kill Wynonie, he's running off at top speed, laughing like a maniac.

C.C. Rider: Little Esther Phillips

The old farm truck was bouncing and straining at the seams. I had a load of live chickens I had planned to drop off at the old Feed and Grain store, but when I got there it was closed. Now I had to keep going to the Barrelhouse Club, chickens and all. It was talent show night at the club, and I was running late.

As I went speeding down the rough road, I could see the faint glow of the Barrelhouse parking lot lights ahead. With the truck bumping up and down, the chickens squawking, and the old engine groaning, I could hear the faint sounds of music. I wasn't close enough to tell if I was hearing blues or gospel refrains. Next door to the Barrelhouse was a sanctified church. From a distance, it was often difficult to determine where the rhythms were coming from. But if you got close enough, you could separate the club sounds from the church. If you heard the word "baby" a lot it was the club. If you heard "Jesus," it was the church.

Okay, I could hear it now, "Baby, where'd you stay last night?" It had to be the Barrelhouse. At times, though, when the church and the club were rockin' at the same time, you might hear a wonderful mish-mash of tambourines, saxophones, organ, guitar, and drums mixed with "Can I get a witness for Jesus?" and "Can I get little lovin', baby?"

Because I was so late, I pulled into the parking lot too fast. I hit a big rock and knocked a couple chicken crates off the truck. The crates broke open and spilled chickens all over the parking lot.

"Never mind the chickens," Bobby Nunn yelled, "We'll catch 'em. You go ahead in 'cause you're late!

As I walked in, the band was rockin'. Kansas City Bell was singing "Wee Baby Blues," and the dance floor was packed. It was 1949, and the Barrelhouse Club was at the peak of its popularity. Our Thursday night talent shows, with popular disc jockey Hunter Hancock as master of ceremonies, were always standing-room only affairs.

As the talent show began, Hunter called me to the microphone. "Johnny," he said, "All week long you've been raving to me about a new young girl singer you've discovered."

"Yeah, Hunter, I found her singing down on 103rd. Street at the Largo Theatre. I want you all to hear her tonight, here she is, Little Esther Jones."

Esther sang the blues, the crowd went nuts, and that night, thirteen-year-old Little Esther (later known as Esther Phillips) began her historic, bittersweet career. I don't describe that night as the start of her "climb" to success, because our first record with Esther ("Double Crossing Blues") was a smash and it catapulted her to instant stardom. She instantly became the teenage favorite among Black music lovers. Everywhere we went, from coast to coast, thousands of adoring fans lined up to see and hear Little Esther.

In spite of all the excitement and adulation in her life during that time, I sensed a wistful sadness under the surface with Esther. Our relationship was often stormy. She could be an exasperating little bitch at times, and I know I can be a pain in the ass, too. But in spite of all that, we became trusting friends. As time went by, she began to unfold

Johnny Otis, Little Esther, and Mel Walker.

From left to right, front row: T-Bone Walker, Shuggie Otis, Little Esther Phillips, Lowell Fulson, and Roy Milton. Back row: Johnny Otis and Charles Brown. At the KNET-TV studios, Los Angeles, 1969. Photo by Steve LaVere, copyright 1993, Mimosa Records Prod., Inc.

a story of unrequited love and heartache in her earlier life that left me flabbergasted. Flabbergasted because here she was, barely fourteen years old, with a history of experiences that would more typically belong to some worldly forty-year-old woman.

The story she told me had its beginning at a revival meeting near Houston, Texas. She sang a gospel song at a service and caught the eye of the handsome circuit riding preacher who ran the revival. He seduced her that night and Esther wound up with a king-size crush on him. She attended every service that week. She tried desperately to gain his attention again but to no avail. He had used her, and now was no longer interested.

She said, "Johnny, I followed that cold-hearted man like I was a little puppy. I practically threw myself at his feet, but I was just a nuisance to him, he just brushed me aside like I was dirt. What made matters worse, with almost every sermon, he preached against blues music and blues singers. He called the blues the devil's music. He said everyone connected with the devil's music was going to burn in hell. I felt so confused and guilty because I idolized Dinah Washington and I wanted to be a blues singer. On top of it all, I was miserable because I had a crush on him. One night, I hung around outside the tent after the service hoping to see him. After a while, all the people were gone, and the electric lights went out. I went around to the back of the tent where he had his dressing room, and I peeked through a crack in the canvas. He was lying on a mattress on the floor with one of the women in the choir. They were smoking pot and drinking whiskey. As he took her in his arms, she reached up and turned off the kerosene lamp on the table. I was shocked! I was crushed! I ran through the night and cried. I ran and cried. I wanted to die! What I saw should've cured me of him, but you know what? If that nigger showed up right now, I'd probably collapse and go to him."

Esther's fame grew, and as time went by, people everywhere recognized her by sight. The preacher used the name Reverend Daniel D. Upholder, but his real name was Willard Dillingsworth. One early morning, as our bus drove through the outskirts of Jackson, Mississippi, we passed a tent with a large sign on it that read, REV. DANIEL D. UPHOLDER REVIVAL HERE NOW! Esther sat straight up in her seat as we drove by. Most of the people on the bus were asleep, and Esther glanced back to see if I was awake. She looked at me for a long moment, then turned away. She knew I had seen the sign. And even if I hadn't, her mother exclaimed, "Oh, Esther, Reverend Upholder is here the same time we are, remember him?"

Redd Foxx, Johnny Otis, Little Esther Phillips (thirteen years old), and Slappy White. The Johnny Otis Show, Royal Theatre, Baltimore, 1950.

Wilton Felder, Johnny Otis, Little Esther Phillips, Paul Lagos, and Shuggie Otis. At the KNET-TV studios, Los Angeles, 1969. Photo by Steve LaVere, copyright 1993, Mimosa Records Prod., Inc.

Esther rolled her eyes at me and answered dryly, "Yeah, I remember him."

"Girl, I wish you wouldn't act so sacrilegious," her mother snapped, "You gettin' just like Johnny Otis and Mario! It's ugly to disrespect God's messengers, and God don't like ugly."

"Lucille, what you bitchin' about now?" our bass player Mario Delagarde asked.

"I'm talkin' about God's preachers, we should have a real commitment to them."

"Horseshit!" Mario the avowed atheist said under his breath.

Real commitment! Don't worry, Lucille, I thought, some of us have a real commitment to preachers, and you'd be surprised who, and how real!

Lady Dee Williams, Von Streeter, and Johnny Otis. Devonia (Lady Dee) Williams played with Big Jay McNeely's Band as well as with Johnny Otis. Her Dee Williams Sextet recorded the hit "Bongo Blues" in 1949.

I didn't see the preacher while we were in Jackson, but I'm sure he and Esther saw each other. The morning we pulled out of Jackson, Esther's tutor Mrs. Jordan said, "My, that was a handsome older man you were talking to in the cafe this morning."

"Yeah," Esther replied, "One of my teachers from Watts."

"Oh, I would've loved to talk to him."

"Well, he was in a hurry."

Esther shot me a quick glance, and I figured that C.C. Rider had struck again. Months later, Esther told me how the preacher would follow the band from town to town and how she had been slipping off to be with him. Now that she was famous and had money, the fact that Esther was singing the blues didn't bother him.

"He don't talk about that Devil's music stuff no more," Esther said.

"I guess not, he smells money," I said, expecting her to become defensive, but it seemed she had had enough of him.

"Yeah, you're right," she said, "but I was getting sick of him before he started begging me for money."

"I wonder if he knows the devil ain't nothing compared to what he'll get if the authorities ever find him laying up with a fifteen-year-old girl?" I muttered.

A few months later, while we were in Chicago, Esther introduced me to the preacher. As we were saying our hello's, she started laughing. The good reverend was puzzled, but I knew how crass Esther could be at times. She was looking right at me going, "Ha-ha-ha!" real loud, which meant, "This is the motherfucker I used to chase after, now he's chasing me!"

When I established the Landmark Church in Los Angeles, Esther was one of the first people to become a member. Her excessive drinking had begun to affect her health, and whenever she was in Los Angeles, she'd come to see me. I did my best to help her to conquer her alcohol problem, but I could see her losing weight and looking weaker by the day.

A doctor called me from Washington, D.C., to tell me he was sending Esther back to Los Angeles in the middle of an engagement because she was in such bad shape.

"I know she does drugs, but it's the alcohol that will kill her if she doesn't stop drinking . . . her liver is shot," he told me.

The Rose Room in Jackson, Mississippi, was an Art Deco style room with a glass-brick dance floor and neon lights inside that caused the floor to glow a beautiful red and green. We checked into a rooming house the morning we arrived in Jackson. We stayed there whenever we were in Jackson, just as many other bands and gospel groups did. That afternoon, I met Sam Cooke who was traveling as lead singer with the Soul Stirrers.

"I'm glad to meet you, Sam," I said. "I've been enjoying your work on records, and now it's nice to meet you in person."

"Thanks, Johnny, I really like your records too," he replied.

"Hey Sam, you know that's the Devil's music you talkin' about," I said jokingly.

We had a laugh and he said, "Oh, I don't believe that old-time stuff. I think the blues is beautiful."

"Well, if you ever decide to record some popular-style music, I'd like to be your producer."

"Thanks, I'll keep that in mind," Sam said.

Knowing that he was in the gospel field, I asked him if he knew of Reverend Daniel D. Upholder. Sam chuckled. "You mean ole Reverend Dan D. Upholder? Dan D. as in Dandy? That's what some people call him, Reverend Dandy, but not to his face."

A friend of mine who lived in Jackson chimed in with "The D stands for DAWG! Man, this cat is the original C.C. Rider. He comes to town once a year, sets up his tent, talks that talk, takes all the money, heals some shills he got planted in the congregation, and does the Three *F*'s on the good-lookin' sisters."

"The Three *F*'s?" I asked.

"Yeah, fool'em, fuck'em, and forget'em, ha, ha, ha!"

The day before Esther passed away, I visited her in the hospital. She was laying there asleep, looking frail and gaunt. I reached over and patted her hand, and she stirred. She reached over for her glasses. I had never noticed how thick the lenses were.

"Don't bother with your glasses, baby, just rest." I said.

"Oh hi, Johnny," she said in a tiny voice, "gimmie a hug, sugar."

As I leaned toward her, my mind raced back in time. I remembered the bright-eyed, brash, talented little girl I had found in Watts years ago, and a big sob welled up in me.

"Don't cry, baby," she said softly, but I cried all the way home.

I conducted her funeral service just as she had instructed me. "No crying and bullshit eulogies. Just my friends singing and playing and having a party."

As the people filed by to view the body, I looked up to see Reverend Daniel D. Upholder—older, grayer, but still strikingly handsome. We nodded to each other, and as he stood by the casket looking down at Esther, a big tear rolled down his cheek.

At that moment, I could almost hear Esther singing,

"Oh, C., C.C. Rider

See What You Have Done. . . . ."

PART 4

THE MUSIC

Music and Politics

I find it impossible to separate a discussion of rhythm and blues from the social and political factors that bear on the African American people who invented the music. A few members of my inner circle have hinted that I should temper my more controversial views for fear that I may offend certain powerful whites or that I may disturb those blacks who are edgy about rocking the boat. To begin with, there are no powerful whites who are concerned about what Johnny Otis has to say or, for that matter, who even know who I am. And as far as edgy blacks are concerned . . . so what? They needn't worry. Mister Charlie's not going to get them. This is me talking. At age seventy, I am not about to start manicuring my remarks to keep from rankling someone. I didn't worry about what people might think when I was twenty years old, and I don't give a shit now.

What I do care about is someday realizing the American Dream of equality, brotherhood, and justice . . . a proposition that is as far from reality today as it was in the days of my youth. I am concerned about my people . . . African Americans . . . who are held hostage by a hostile white majority. I am disgusted that our country is the only advanced nation in the world without universal health coverage . . . that we have the highest infant mortality rate . . . the largest population of homeless people, and the most obscene misdistribution of wealth. I am worried about our third-rate educational system . . . the fact that one- fourth of our young Black men are imprisoned, on parole, or on probation.

We have a drug blight eating away at the heart of America, and all our government can come up with is a slogan-ridden, bullshit "War on Drugs." A war that in the final analysis, translates into a war on Black people. The United States holds a mere five percent of the world's population but consumes fifty percent of all illegal drugs. These facts define

Johnny Otis, Lady Dee Williams, and George Washington at the Paradise Theatre in Detroit, 1950.

an ailing society. Jazz great Charles Mingus had it right all along, "This goddamn country is sick!" Every sociopolitical disease that afflicts the United States hits hardest at African Americans. These are the people who created blues, jazz, rhythm and blues, swing, rock and roll, so called Dixieland, bebop, and so on and on and on. In these pages, I intend to trace, to the best of my ability, the history and development of rhythm and blues music with an emphasis on the Central Avenue brand of R&B, that Los Angeles musical revolution that I was fortunate to be part of and that I have firsthand knowledge of. No one has appointed, designated, or elected me any kind of spokesman. I speak for no one nor do I represent anyone but myself.

Big Joe, Cleanhead, and Bones

During the forties and fifties, Big Joe Turner, Eddie "Cleanhead" Vinson, and T-Bone Walker were out on the road, touring with their own bands. We saw one another from time to time, in one city or another, and occasionally we worked on the same bill together. But by 1970, all three were performing as solo acts. In one extended period during those years, they all worked together in my show. After T-Bone passed away, Cleanhead and Joe worked with me up into the eighties. To have all three of these creative blues giants in the show at one time was really something. It was like a reunion party for Big Jim Wynn, Mighty Flea, and myself, and a valuable learning experience for the young people in the group.

All three had the unfortunate habit of drinking too much. In the early days, before the deadly effects of alcohol abuse were as widely known and understood as they are today, hard drinking was associated with partying, having a good time, making good music. We didn't know much about the health hazards connected with overdrinking then.

> JOE: "Hey Bones, pass that bottle to me."
> CLEANHEAD: "When YOU gonna buy a bottle?"
> JOE: "Ain't no need me buyin' when everybody else is buyin'."
> T-BONE: "You gonna drink yourself into bad health."
> JOE: "I'm gonna' keep drinkin to everyone's health, 'til I ruin my own."

It didn't matter that they were reciting comedian Dusty Fletcher's gags, they were partying, and damn the consequences.

In my experience, most pot smokers can get high and function credibly, but the heavy drug users and the drunks are a pathetic mess. They are a big headache to whomever hires them. Bone, Cleanhead, and Joe Turner were exceptions. No matter how intoxicated they were, they could still go up to the mike and perform well. Cleanhead was the most

At the KNET-TV studios in Los Angeles, 1969, from left to right: Wilton Felder (bass), Johnny Otis (piano), Big Joe Turner (vocal), Paul Lagos (drums). Rear line: Melvin Moore (trumpet) and Gene "Mighty Flea" Conners (trombone). Front line: Preston Love (baritone sax) and Plas Johnson (tenor sax). Photo by Steve LaVere, copyright 1993, Mimosa Records Prod., Inc.

amazing of the three. He could be sloppy drunk and still blow his horn and sing great. In the end, though, no matter how well they balanced their drinking and performing, they weren't made of steel, and the alcohol took its toll.

Many of our important R&B performers had a drinking problem. On the other hand, many did not. Charles Brown, Joe Liggins, Roy Milton, Ruth Brown, and Louis Jordan, just to name a few, were never known to be heavy drinkers, if they drank at all. But alcoholism claimed Little Esther Phillips's and Big Mama Thornton's lives. Drug addiction certainly didn't help Esther's health, but it was her liver and kidneys ruined by alcohol that caused her death at age 47. Being an African American in an anti-Black society is not something that everyone can cope with. So, a legitimate question is were Big Joe, Cleanhead, and T-Bone partying, or were they trying to drown their misery?

Now that peddling drugs has become a way for many ghetto inhabitants to make money, a drug culture has developed. The reaction on the part of the establishment has not been to deal with the causes of this problem but, rather, to react as they've always reacted in similar situations: that is, to rail against the effects, which include addiction, killings, crack, gangs, and guns. But the crux of the drug problem is not about crack, gangs, and guns, it is about people and poverty and hopelessness. It is not about a War on Drugs, which translates into a war on the inner cities, which boils down to a war on Black people. There should not be a mad rush to build more prisons, to punish more people. There should be a massive effort to eliminate the conditions that produce overcrowded prisons. There has been too much punishment. More punishment would compound the cruelty and do nothing

Big Joe Turner (1911–1985) remains best known for his twenty best-selling rhythm and blues records between 1946 and 1958, especially "Shake, Rattle, and Roll," "Honey Hush," "Chains of Love," and "Corrine Corrina."

to solve the problem. The drug problem grows out of neglect, grinding poverty, and dead-end lives. The drug problem and the many other social ills that grow out of racism are not going to be corrected by more cracking of victim's heads and spirits. America must attend to the long-deferred business of treating all human beings as human beings. At the present, there seems little chance of this happening. If we don't cure this problem, however, sooner or later, it is going to blow up in our face.

The Bassackwards Blues

Something as powerful as blues music naturally attracts artists from both inside and outside the culture. But when the music grows out of a unique way of life and it reflects the inside workings of a particular people, as the blues does, then it certainly follows that artists within that culture will function in a freer and more natural manner, and, no matter how skilled the emulator, he or she will never get it quite right. Eddie "Cleanhead" Vinson used to say that white performers, and particularly the singers, had the blues "Bassackwards." This doesn't mean of course, that the world perceives or understands the qualitative difference. This goes for the so-called experts and critics as well as the average person. After all, the music industry and the pop audience go hog-wild over The Rolling Stones, Elvis Presley, Janis Joplin, and the Beatles, while not having nearly the same level of appreciation for a Lloyd Price, a Ruth Brown, or an Otis Redding, or, for that matter, Aretha Franklin or Ray Charles.

Today, all over the country, there are dozens of white "blues" bands. They are busy churning out enthusiastic parodies of Muddy Waters, Howlin' Wolf, Little Walter, and so on. Almost all of the young Black blues performers of the present day are pathetically bland compared to the powerhouse men and women of the thirties, forties, and fifties. The same holds true for the "soul" performers of the sixties as compared to today's African American pop performers. The music establishment accepts the white copy cat and the lukewarm Black performer without any misgivings. The older, more traditional Black blues singers and players view today's blues scene with bemusement and regret, and often with bitterness. The bitterest pill of all, however, is the fact that the Black culture itself has largely abandoned its musical heritage.

It has been said that "what goes around, comes around." If I have a

From left: Ahmet Ertegun, Joe Turner, and Jerry Wexler of Atlantic Records.

fond wish, it is to see, before I die, what comes around as blues and jazz go around again. I do not suggest that the new generation of artistic men and women should create and perform exactly as the traditional founders did. What I would love to see someday, though, is a strong movement among budding Black talents to build upon and carry on the glorious tradition of blues and jazz artistry. After all, although it bears scant resemblance to the early African American community that thrilled the world with musical brilliance, it is still the African American community. There just have to be some potential Louis Armstrongs, Duke Ellingtons, Ray Charles, Dinah Washingtons, B. B. Kings, and Count Basies in the gene pool.

It Don't Mean a Thing
if It Ain't Got That Swing

One afternoon, in the early days of R&B, Joe Liggins and I wandered into a Central Avenue night club. We hadn't expected to run into him, but there was Roy Milton up on the bandstand adjusting his drum set. There wasn't anyone else around, just Roy getting his traps together. Later that night, the room would be full of people having a good time. Spotlights and neon signs would be flashing, and the place would come alive with music and dancing. At the moment, however, in the cold light of day, the club was lifeless—and tacky. Frayed carpets, worn chair cushions, and that sour beer smell that is so typical of barrooms in the daytime. I've never experienced that smell at night, only in the daytime.

Roy didn't notice us. Look at him, I thought, a little nondescript, bald, not-so-young guy. To look at him, you wouldn't get a hint of the magic he would conjure up later that night. He resembled a night watchman or janitor more than the popular entertainer he was. That night however, he'd come into the club in style, formal lamé jacket glittering, hairpiece in place, smiling from ear to ear. He'd sit down at his drums, kick his band into overdrive, and the good times would roll. "Why, oh why," he'd croon, "Why did you break my heart?" At that point, it wouldn't matter how tattered the carpet or how frayed the cushions, or how many beers had been spilled on the carpet. Who would notice the sour beer odor with the sweet aroma of pure rhythm and blues in the air?

Roy finally spotted us and called out, "Hey, fellas, what's happenin'?" He pointed at his drum set and said, "I'm gettin' me a drummer, then all I gotta do is show up at the gig. No wrestling with a damn drum set. You know, jut walk in and sing. You piano players got it made, Joe. But me and Johnny gotta lug these tubs all over the place!" At the time,

Roy and I were still playing drums in our bands. It wasn't long before Roy hired a drummer and concentrated on vocals and I switched from drums to piano and vibes.

As a drummer, Roy had his detractors. Some musicians thought he wasn't technically slick enough. I always thought he was just fine. He didn't have to be Max Roach or Jo Jones to play his brand of music. All he had to do was rock that little rhythm and blues band of his, and he knew just how to do that. The same kind of debate went on in Duke Ellington's band. Some of Duke's men (and certain "sidewalk superintendent" types outside the band) felt that Sonny Greer didn't swing enough in the "modern way." Some really fine drummers followed Sonny in Duke's band, but Sonny Greer was always special to the Ellington sound. "Cotton Tail" and "Harlem Air Shaft" are just two records that demonstrate the galloping, loping, rocking rhythm that Sonny Greer brought to the world of African American music. It sure sounds like he's swinging to me.

The world of jazz snobbery decided who would be considered valid, and who would be deemed flawed. Jessie Price, Kid Lips Hackett, and Gus Johnson were wonderful drummers, but they seldom received any serious acclaim. If propelling a band with great feeling and rhythmic vitality were important elements in the swing/jazz field, these men, and

Johnny Otis and the Otisettes. From left to right: Otis, Lisa, "Stuff," and Terisa.

Roy Milton and Al Jarvis circa 1946. Born in Wynnewood, Oklahoma, in 1907, Milton moved to Los Angeles in the 1930s. He fused jump blues and gospel sounds in his band, Roy Milton and his Solid Senders. Milton had nineteen Top Ten rhythm and blues hits between 1946 and 1953. His "R.M. Blues" stayed on the charts for twenty-five weeks in 1946.

Jarvis was one of the first white disc jockeys to feature selections by black artists on his radio programs.

others like them, were invaluable. Kid Lips Hackett was summarily dismissed as a "real" jazz drummer, probably because of his flashy act of tossing the drum sticks around, bouncing them off the floor, holding sticks in his mouth as he juggled others in the air, and the like. It seems the official appraisers of jazz and swing felt that showmanship gimmicks could not be part of a genuine artist's arsenal. Preston Love recalls a night with the Basie band when Kid Lips sat in and delighted the band with his swinging power. The Basie men agreed that next to Jo Jones, Kid Lips generated the most excitement in the band.

Jessie Price and Gus Johnson didn't employ any flashy gimmicks, just plain old grooving power. The early R&B drummers borrowed from Price and Johnson. Jimmy Lunceford's great rhythm master, James Crawford, was an important role model. The evolving R&B concept required straight 4/4, afterbeat, and steady shuffle rhythms. Highly technical and fancy modern jazz drummers were usually unsuited to the new music. In fact, it was difficult to get the average bebop-schooled drummer to lay down a steady pulse beat. The frills, bombs, and embellishments got in the way of the straight-ahead rhythm patterns that were the foundation for jump blues.

When I decided to move from drums to piano, finding a drummer who would play a strong, uncomplicated backbeat style became a problem. The average young drummers of the day either had contempt for the new blues-based music or were too conditioned to dropping bombs and embellishments to ever settle down to the business of a steady groove.

Once my Watts-based Barrelhouse Club was open and established, blues singers and musicians, both famous and unknown, were constantly dropping by to sit in. Two young men would often come up and trade choruses on jump blues à la vintage Big Joe Turner. One night, I was called off the bandstand, and one of the fellows sat down and took over the drums. At that moment, I knew I had found my human rhythm machine. His name was Leard Bell, and he hailed from Kansas City. I dubbed him Kansas City Bell, and the nickname stuck. He was in his twenties, arms like a weight lifter, with a rock-solid style that fit my band of the late forties-early fifties to a tee. He was to become a personal buddy, and a dear and loyal friend.

In the late fifties, as R&B music became more rhythmically challenging, I reorganized my band, including musicians who were able to read music and execute the new musical developments with ease. Unfortunately, the new band could not include Bell. This was the most heartwrenching decision of my musical life. Bell has not spoken to me since. I understand his hurt. I wish it could have been otherwise. I love him a lot, and although it was unavoidable, I feel guilty as hell.

The young singer who traded blues choruses with Bell was a fellow named Bobby Nunn who hung around the Barrelhouse. He was the man who teamed up with Little Esther on the big 1950 hit, "Double Crossing Blues." I added him to the A Sharp Trio, a vocal group that won a 1949 Barrelhouse talent show contest. They became The Robins, and, later, Bobby Nunn was to sing the famous bass voice on the Coasters' smash "Charlie Brown."

With the exception of a few sides that I played on, Kansas City Bell played drums on all our early fifties records. I never had to ask him to keep the beat simple. He was not inclined to try to get fancy, which was a blessing to me. Duke Ellington's admonition that, "It Don't Mean a Thing if It Ain't Got That Swing," seems to have escaped many avant-garde musicians. Today's jazz players tend to be technical wizards and academy trained, mile-a-minute note dispensers. But generally speaking, most of what passes for jazz today flies in the face of African American tradition. In other words, it don't mean a thing if it ain't got that swing.

Before his passing, jazz great Art Blakey complained bitterly that, "All my people want to do is finger-pop." To a great degree, that's true, but then, all anybody's people want to do is finger-pop, finger-pop, and party. No one in their right mind could ever accuse Art Blakey's fine bands of not swinging. In the best of times, unfortunately, quality ensembles such as Blakey's Jazz Messengers do not fill large arenas the way that R&B stars such as Aretha Franklin, Ray Charles, B. B. King, or James Brown have been able to do. These are no less fine artists than Art Blakey. The one difference being, they satisfy the audience's urge to finger-pop. Dizzy Gillespie, with his warm and wonderful stage manner, replete with dance steps and vocals, gives the average audience a lot to hang on to, even if his highly advanced music sails right over most of their heads.

Art Blakey hated the fact that Black audiences had abandoned traditional Black jazz music. Of course, the same sad fact exists for all traditional Black music. That includes swing, country blues, rock and roll, rhythm and blues, New Orleans (so-called Dixieland) music, boogie-woogie, ragtime, stride piano, and, of course, bebop and modern jazz. Our audiences today are practically all white. Thank God for paying customers of whatever color, of course, but when there are Black people in the audience, African American performers get a special lift. The music takes on a heightened character. White rhythm and blues audiences can be enthusiastic and animated, but it's not the same. With a Black audience the crowd becomes part of the performance in a very unique way. Much as in the Black church, a call and response often develops, and Black magic fills the air. That kind of special finger-popping doesn't happen often nowadays for our band. Nor, I suspect, for other traditional Black groups. In the rare instances when it does, we are transported back in time to the Barrelhouse in Watts, where finger-popping was the order of the day and everyone understood "it don't mean a thing if it ain't got that swing."

Music and African American Life

Touring my band through the Deep South during the forties and fifties was a never-to-be-forgotten experience. I used to marvel at how Black people who lived there full-time were able to bear up under the constant humiliation and danger of state-sanctioned segregation. Visiting southern cities as Black performers from the North was, in a way, more perilous than being a permanent resident. Our buses usually had New York or California license plates, and this seemed to infuriate the white cops. The dances we played were usually policed by whites, and woe to any one of us who failed to say "yes, sir" to some cracker cop in the bowels of Mississippi!

Even more dangerous than forgetting to say "yes, sir" was using the "whites only" water fountains or rest rooms. Little Esther had a condition that is often referred to as "weak kidneys." When she had to go, she had to go RIGHT NOW and no messing around! Our bus drivers knew when Esther shouted, "I gotta go!" to pull in at the next gas station. One day in the Deep South, she shouted, the driver pulled over, and she flew out of the bus door like a shot. A few minutes later, as I stepped off the bus, the station attendant, trembling with rage, put a revolver to my stomach and snarled, "Get that black bitch outta the white ladies' toilet!" As we finally pulled away, I shuddered to think I could've been shot in the gut because a child who had trouble controlling her bladder in her haste to find a rest room had violated a Jim Crow law.

With open racism holding forth in the South, it's a wonder that blues music contained as much joy and exuberance as it did. Melancholy sounds and lyrics were everywhere in the music, but just as often, the joy of living, sexuality, and wit were the dominant themes. I always got the feeling that the blues poets refused to wallow in despair or self-pity. They seemed to be saying, "Yes, it's rough, but it won't always be this way, and I'm not gonna lay down and roll over."

Johnny Otis and Langston Hughes, 1960. The great poet, author, and playwright often acknowledged his debt to the inspiration and insight he received from Black popular music.

In gardening, some plants are more transplantable than others. On our small farm in Northern California, my son Nicky and I have learned that lettuce and tomatoes can be started indoors and easily replanted in the garden when the weather warms up. Melons and beans, on the other hand, are best sown directly in the garden. The blues is a most transplantable item. Southern Black people moving north brought the seeds of the blues with them. Their children, nurtured in the blues and gospel environment of their transplanted families, carried on the southern musical traditions.

Count Basie, the dominant figure of Kansas City Swing, a musical style drenched in the blues, was from Red Bank, New Jersey. Duke Ellington's first ballads bore the unmistakable stamp of New Orleans. Duke himself, of course, was from Washington, D.C. Seven of the musicians in my first band, Devonia Williams, Walter Henry, Don Johnson, Lorenzo Holden, Mel Walker, Mario Delagarde, and I were non-Southerners. I do not point this out to place myself in the Ellington-Basie class, which would be ridiculous, but to point up the transplant factor in our music. Six of us were Californians, and one, Mario, was

Johnny Otis with the great singer Ella Fitzgerald. Fitzgerald joined the Chick Webb Band in 1934 when she was sixteen. In addition to her extraordinary performances with big bands, Fitzgerald also had hits in the 1940s with Louis Jordan's Tympany Five, the Ink Spots, Bill Doggett, and the Delta Rhythm Boys.

from the Caribbean. The remaining five, Little Esther Phillips, Redd Lyte, Kansas City Bell, Pete Lewis, and George Washington, were from the South. The varied home bases of the individual performers did not create any musical dichotomy within the group. What we played was mostly the blues. We didn't particularly discuss it, or dissect it, or vote on it. We just felt it and played accordingly. We had the blues/gospel environment of the Black community in common. With the Southerners among us, that environment was their childhood days in the downhome, cradle of the blues. With the rest of us, it was our life in the transplanted Black cultures of the North.

I never had to instruct my horn players how to phrase a passage. I never found it necessary to suggest to one of my singers how a song should be handled. I just equipped them with the words or notes, and they supplied the all-important elements. The whole flavor of traditional African American culture came to bear on their interpretations. The essence of traditional Black singing and playing and the way the artistry was spun out had to do with more than mere lyrics or melodies, or saxophones or guitars. It had to do with the way Black folks lived and were raised in their homes. The music grew out of the African American way of life. The way mama cooked, the Black English grandmother and grandfather spoke, the way daddy disciplined the kids—the emphasis in spiritual values, the way Reverend Jones preached, the way Sister Williams sang in the choir, the way the old brother down the street played the slide guitar and crooned the blues, the very special way the people danced, walked, laughed, cried, joked, got happy, shouted in church. In the final analysis, what forms the texture and adds character to the music is the African American experience. That experience runs the gamut from the blessings of American life (and there are many) to the brutal pressures of a racist system. No one in their right mind can suggest that what Black people have had to endure at the hands of white racists is a good thing because the suffering imparted a powerful melancholy element to the music. At the same time, the trials and tribulations have made their mark on the artistry. Having to listen to—and sometimes be required to recite—such high-minded phrases as "With Liberty and Justice for All," and knowing silently that it was so much bullshit, probably contributed notes of irony to the art of the blues.

Discipline and Style

The big band culture of the thirties and forties set the stage for the discipline in the R&B bands of the fifties and sixties. In the early big swing bands, deportment and appearance were stressed along with musicianship. By the seventies, all that had changed. Formal and semiformal uniforms were replaced by a go-for-yourself dress code. The new band attire ran the gamut from raggedy jeans and T-shirt to outrageous sequin and feathered outfits. Wild costumes, fantastic stage sets, flashing lights, smoke bombs, and choreography counted for more than vocal talent or gifted musicianship with the advent of videos. In front of the television camera, youth, beauty, and skillful dancing took precedence over artistry. More and more singers tended to be mediocre. There were, and still are, exceptions, of course, but not many.

If they had to start out now, Billie Holiday, Carmen McRae, Bessie Smith, Dinah Washington, Ella Fitzgerald, Ruth Brown, Little Esther Phillips, Laverne Baker, Etta James, Koko Taylor, Aretha Franklin, and Gladys Knight would not make it to stardom in today's music world. They would be required to shake their behinds and run all over the stage practically undressed or cheaply overdressed. This anti-artistry behavior would be alien to the great women of traditional Black music.

The Black-territory bands of the pre-fifties years represented more than just a gig to make some bucks with. Those early bands functioned as schools for the singers and musicians who aspired to the big time. To move up from the territory-band category to a Count Basie, Jimmie Lunceford, or Duke Ellington Orchestra was the dream. The older men in the territory bands functioned as mentors and disciplinarians.

As a youngster, I worked in two bands that were typical of the era. Lloyd Hunter's Serenaders out of Omaha, Nebraska, and Harlan Leonard's Kansas City Rockets. When Lloyd Hunter's fine drummer,

At the Club Alabam on Central Avenue in 1945. Top row left to right: John Pettigrew, Jap Allen, and Curtis Counce. Bottom row: Von Streeter and Johnny Otis. At the microphone: Lionel Hampton and Babe Wallace.

Bobby Parker of Des Moines, Iowa, was drafted, I inherited the drum seat. Later, I landed a job with Harlan Leonard's band when the great Jessie Price was called to military service. It was my good luck to be available when Bobby and Jessie were drafted. As a result, I gained first-hand experience on what it was like in the Black-territory band culture. The older men and women of the territory bands acted as role models and teachers to the young musicians starting their climb up the musical ladder.

Time Machine

Sometimes I wish I had a time machine. Then I could take my sons and some of the younger members of my band back to, say, the late thirties or early forties. Our first stop would be 1941 to the Orpheum Theatre in Omaha to see the Count Basie band with all the original members still intact. My son Nicky would see the great Jo Jones as he was in his prime, showing the world what modern drumming was to be all about. Hearing about Papa Jo from someone who was there or listening to the recordings of the original Basie band is one thing, but seeing, hearing and FEELING Jo Jones in person would be another. Why a theatre? Because the acoustics in the old, traditional movie houses captured the sounds of the great swing bands in a unique way. The cathedral-like height of the stage and back stage and the width and breadth of the seating auditorium gave the music a special grand resonance.

Preston Love and I haunted the Orpheum when the great Black bands played there. During one Count Basie engagement, we sat through almost every set, every day. It was just as thrilling during the final show as during the first. Pres and I came up during the Great Depression of the thirties. Both of our families suffered economic disaster during that time, so, we knew what it was to go without. One thing we shared was a love of strawberries and ice cream—something we saw very, very little of during the lean times. When we did luck up on strawberries or ice cream, we savored them slowly, scooping up every last little drop as though we'd never taste that treat again in life. That's how we felt when Duke Ellington or Count Basie or any of the other great Black bands came to town. As the depression eased up and our fortunes improved, we were able to enjoy things like strawberries and ice cream, but the day came when Count Basie and Duke Ellington were gone. Now, we dream of taking our kids on a time trip so they can see and hear what we're always raving about.

Screamin' Jay Hawkins visits Johnny Otis's radio show on KPFK, Los Angeles, 1984. A former boxer and piano player, Hawkins, born in 1929, was best known for his flamboyant stage show and his 1956 hit "I Put A Spell on You."

Preston's sons, Norman and Richie, followed in his footsteps and became saxophone players. Going back in time would give them a peek at Lester Young, Earl Warren, Ben Webster, and Johnny Hodges. My son Shuggie could see Basie's guitarist, Freddy Green, and my grandson, fledgling bassist Lucky (Shuggie's son), would experience the mighty Walter Page. And how valuable it might be to expose some of our current crop of young singers to the understated magic of Billie Holiday or Brook Benton. But for the present-day tendency to overscreech and squall and use ill-advised pop mannerisms and gimmicks, some of our young singers are real talents, blessed with sensational voices and sharp ears. I keep thinking that, given a bit of exposure to unadulterated blues and jazz and a measure of artistic discretion and balance, we could conceivably see the emergence of a crop of young singers in the true tradition of historic African American artistry. You know, like Sarah, Ella, Roy Hamilton, or Charles Brown. I can dream, can't I?

PART 5

PREACHING, PAINTING,

AND PLOWING

Landmark Community Church

In 1950, for a mere $18,000, I bought a fourteen-room mansion in the Los Angeles Sugar Hill district. I had only $1,200 as a down payment, but it was a time of Blacks moving into upscale neighborhoods and whites (in their haste to escape) practically giving these lovely homes away before fleeing to the suburbs. Phyllis and I raised our kids in that great old house on Harvard Boulevard. It was built of imported redwood with large slabs of marble in the bathrooms and silver and crystal chandeliers in the dining area . We could never have afforded such a luxurious home, but prejudice works in mysterious ways. This one time, at least, in our favor.

In the mid-sixties we leased the property and moved to Southwest Los Angeles. In the seventies, I remodeled the old Harvard house, and with a few structural changes, we established the nondenominational Landmark Community Church, where I served as pastor for ten years. Those years have left me with some of the most meaningful memories of my life: our splendid gospel choir under the direction of the late David Pridgen, Charles Williams's sensational vocal solos, the heart-warming fellowship, the happy moments during weddings and baptisms, leaning on one another during funerals and hospital visits, the spirit-filled services, the shouting, the dancing, the pleasure of getting off a well-received sermon, the satisfaction of knowing that our congregation, which was predominantly Black, included some whites, Latinos, and Asians. We had three Jewish members and two Buddhists. They were regular attendees and supporters because they liked the general philosophy—love, forgiveness, brotherhood—and they were not required to forsake their original faith to fellowship with us. This doesn't sit well with most church leaders. They are married to the "ain't nobody goin' to heaven but us" syndrome. And what the hell do I know about heaven?

Johnny, Phyllis, and Shuggie Otis with Rev. H. B. Charles, Mt. Sinai Baptist Church (photo courtesy Abie Robinson).

I know about love and brotherhood, and that's enough. Our followers from other spiritual backgrounds knew this and felt comfortable. Many came to the church out of curiosity. They came to see what Reverend Hand Jive was talking about. Often, first-time visiting non-Blacks were a little dazed and self-conscious at the enthusiastic fervor of a so-called "sanctified" Black church service, but they soon relaxed and enjoyed themselves. Some never left.

The first funeral I conducted was that of Jazz trombonist Henry Coker. In time, I was to hold final services for many musicians and singers, among them Little Esther Phillips, Big Mama Thornton, King

Pleasure, Ernie Freeman, bassist Montudie, Bardu Ali, and others. Members of the congregation included jazz organist Jimmy Smith and his wife Lola, Etta James, Lawanda "Aunt Esther" Page, and many other show business folk.

The most meaningful activity at our church was feeding homeless people. At first, there weren't many groups out there trying to help the homeless, but as time went by, and more people became aware

Pastor Johnny Otis at the Landmark Community Church. Otis used to attend services at the Mount Sinai Missionary Baptist Church. One day, Pastor H. B. Charles pointed to Sam Cooke and Johnny Otis and said that he prayed that one day they would give up "the devil's music and return to the Lord." Cooke leaned over to Otis and whispered "We've got to get out of here." Later, Otis was ordained by a Mother Bernice Smith, a Black female evangelist who felt that he had the calling to head a congregation. Skeptical at first ("You mean, people would listen to sermons from Reverend Hand Jive?" he asked her) Otis founded the Landmark Church and ran it successfully for ten years.

of their plight, additional groups and individuals pitched in. But the efforts never matched the needs. The fact that so many human beings in America are without adequate food, clothing, shelter, medical care, or hope for the future constitutes a national disgrace. I fear that, as more of our country's wealth is concentrated into fewer hands and American corporate fascism becomes more entrenched, the shame in the streets will grow.

Next door to the church was a county home for retarded people. When the weather was nice, I'd keep the window in my office open. Jomo, my African Grey parrot would crawl out on the second story window sill to check out the action below. Often, two old men, one Black and one white, would sit on the side porch of the home and smoke a last cigarette before the lady in charge called them in for the night. Almost always, the white fellow would start howling like a wolf and the little old brother would shout, "Shut up, motherfucker!" Jomo was a great mimic and it wasn't long before he had the phrase down pat. In fact, he'd drop it in on cue as soon as the howling started. He also had the irritating habit of waiting until I'd walked downstairs to call, "Hey Rev!" in my friend Delmar Evans's voice. It was so convincing, I'd bound back upstairs only to realize Jomo had fooled me again. I always had the feeling that the little sucker was enjoying his sly little joke.

The old lady who cleaned up the church offices and living quarters was a sanctified old soul who hummed gospel songs as she tidied up the place. Every now and then, she'd cut loose with "My Soul is a Witness!" It didn't take Jomo long to add that saying to his repertoire. There are many jokes about talking parrots, but never anything more hilarious than what actually happened at the church one day. I was meeting with three sisters on some church business when, from his perch in the corner of my office, Jomo squawked, "My soul is a witness!" The ladies were enchanted. One of them said, "Ooooh, Pastor! You've got a spiritual parrot!" The way she pronounced "Ooooh!" reminded Jomo of the familiar wolf howl, and he barked back, "Shut up, motherfucker!"

Ethiopian Children

Getting the bulk of our Landmark Church membership to respond to the needs of the many homeless people in the Los Angeles area during the 1980s was a problem. Most would contribute a bit of money from time to time, but when it came to being involved in the day-to-day, actual preparation and distribution of food and clothing, I discovered that I only could count on a precious few dedicated individuals. Out of a membership of over 700, I was lucky to have more than twenty or so turn out to do the real work. Becoming the head of a church in my fifties meant I was lacking in the experience that would have prepared me for such a low turnout.

Reverend Louis Carter, pastor of Antioch Baptist Church in Los Angeles, explained that twenty or thirty out of seven hundred was par for the course. "Pastor Johnny," he said, "You're feeding hungry, homeless people every week, and that's fine. Most so-called Christians talk a good game, but when it comes time to really come through, they thin out. All we preachers have to learn that lesson. Don't be disappointed. Just take your twenty, or ten, or even two caring folks and be about your Father's business."

There was one occasion, however, when the church members truly bowled me over by their response.

My close friend, Hal Kronick, a fellow musician and school chum from way back, got a letter from his sister June who had moved to Israel. She asked Hal if he could contribute a few Black dolls for the Black Jewish children who were being brought to Israel from Ethiopia. There were no Black dolls in Israel, she explained, and the children couldn't relate to the white dolls. In fact, they appeared apprehensive about the white dolls, almost afraid of them.

I mentioned this during our next church service, and within two

Nat Turner by Johnny Otis; 3′ × 5′ oil, in the artist's collection.

weeks, we had a veritable mountain of Black dolls. I packaged the dolls in big boxes and was able to transport them from L.A. to Berkeley in our band bus as we had a music gig in the Bay Area that week. Hal sent the boxes to Israel, whereupon his sister sent the church a letter of appreciation describing the joy with which the children accepted the dolls.

During the fifties' fight to desegregate American schools, Thurgood Marshall, who was at that time the attorney heading up the *Brown vs. Board of Education* case before the Supreme Court, presented a bit of evidence that had a strong effect on the Court. As a result of a scientific study conducted by psychologist Kenneth Clark, it was discovered that, when given a choice of a Black doll or a white doll, the overwhelming majority of African American children would choose the white doll, and in rejecting the Black doll, refer to it as "bad."

The Ethiopian youngsters had lived under religious pressure in Africa but had not experienced color prejudice. After all, everyone at home, Jews, Christians, Muslims, Animists, and so on, had been brown-skinned. They felt secure and comfortable with their new Afro dolls. On the other hand, our Black children here in America, having been bombarded by color bias from the cradle, had, and still have, a distorted sense of self-worth. Damaging innocent children in this way is surely as cruel as a color-conscious society can get.

Ed Soesman, the head deacon of our church, had a theory on why we had such a sensational response to our call for Black dolls. "Although African Americans have become mayors, congresspersons, and even senators," Soesman said, "most of us are still at the bottom of the socioeconomic ladder, still shunned and degraded, strangers in our own country. But when we send little dolls to the Black Hebrew children, who are the offspring of an ancient culture dating back hundreds of years, whose people have been practicing Judaism in Ethiopia since biblical times, a tiny part of us goes back to the motherland with the dolls, even though we are, in fact, sending the dolls to Israel. We can't go back to Africa, of course, nor do we really want to. But the feeling is there."

Draw Me a Picture

Drawing cartoons to make the members of the band laugh is something I've done for many years. In the early fifties, Little Esther Phillips kept me busy sketching things for her. "Draw me this, draw me that." At first, she wanted me to draw things we saw as the band bus moved through the countryside—a barn, a cow, a horse, and so forth. One day, she got into a bitter argument with our bus driver, Little Arthur Matthews, who would later become one of our featured novelty performers. She plopped into the seat next to mine in a great rage. Arthur had gotten the best of her in a shouting match, and she was furious.

"Johnny, draw me a picture of that little funky-butt nigger . . . and make it ugly!" she hissed.

When I hesitated, she grabbed the pencil and drew a cartoon of an outrageous caricature driving a bus with Johnny Otis Band written on it. The cartoon character she came up with was a cross between Barney Google's Mush Mouth and Felix the Cat. In today's world, most people would consider a drawing like that politically incorrect, but the dammned thing was funny as hell, and while it didn't actually look anything like Little Arthur, everyone knew it was supposed to be him because it was driving the bus. At first she wrote, "Evil little ugly motherfucker" on the cartoon but I talked her into changing it to, "Lil' Booger." The people on the bus roared with laughter, and Little Arthur, with his good sense of humor, laughed along with everyone else.

That day, the tradition of my drawing cartoons to amuse the band members was born. Esther started it, but she was never able to come up with anything close to her "Lil' Booger" masterpiece, and I was elected official lampoon cartoonist of the band. Almost every day, someone would come to me with a request for a cartoon. They were usually based on what had happened during or after the gig the night before. Some of the subject matter was benign, but more often the requests were naughty and ranged from erotic to downright pornographic. Occasionally, someone would come to me with great bitterness and order up a vengeance cartoon. Like the time bassist Albert Winston asked me to do a cartoon of Big Mama Thornton. They had had a scuffle and actually came to blows. Big Mama was getting the best of it, but we pulled them apart before any real harm was done.

Winston was seething. "Okay, now get this shit straight. Give me a cartoon of a big, fat pig wallowing in the mud and put her face on it, and make sure it looks just like the bitch!"

Eddie Cleanhead Vinson (1917–1988) played alto saxophone, sang the blues, and led bands during the heyday of rhythm and blues. He had hit records in the late 1940s with "Ole Maid Boogie," "Kidney Stew Blues," and "Somebody Done Stole My Cherry Red." He worked with Milt Larkin, Big Bill Broonzy, and Cootie Williams, and frequently played the Club Alabam and the Orpheum Theatre in Los Angeles.

Johnny Otis with grandchildren, left to right: Gamel, Kevin, and Saran Johnson (courtesy Stephan Rockwerk).

"Wait a minute," I said. "I don't want to get in this mess." Willie Mae and I were good friends, and I didn't need her to throw one of her 300 pound right hooks at me.

"I'll pay you for it . . . you name it!" he shouted.

I'm still knocking out an occasional cartoon for the people in the show. From time to time, "Lil' Booger" is resurrected. As I visited artist supply stores to buy sketch pads and drawing pencils, I began to get interested in the oil paints and all the beautiful colors that were available. In the early sixties, I bought some oils and canvas and started trying to paint. When I first saw photos of West African sculptures and Picasso paintings, I was enthralled. During the seventies, I stopped painting. In the eighties, I started again with wood carving and painting. By picking the brains of fellow artists Charles Dickson and John Outterbridge, I learned of the basics of plaster of Paris and Ultra-Cal 30 sculpture. Since then, I've developed a style of sculpture that I use in my "chair" pieces and things like the life-size work I call The Three Muses. The Muses were inspired by my R&B singing group The Three Tons of Joy. I wanted to use them as models for The Muses but while Doris and Millie seemed game to do it, Marie Adams, the lead singer was much too modest to pose in the nude.

A fellow preacher gave me a set of tiny chairs to use for my children's Sunday School class. Our church youngsters didn't like the little chairs. "We wanna' sit in the big chairs," they complained. So, there I was, stuck

Sonny Boy by Johnny Otis; 3′ × 5′ oil, in the artist's collection.

with 30 miniature chairs. One day, on a whim, I fashioned a plaster of Paris sculpture in one of the chairs and painted it and the chair in bright colors. I enjoyed doing it so much that I made a room full, all different. One day, publicist Veronica Aiken saw them, and she became my art agent. I was sure this would be an exercise in futility, but she began selling the stuff, and I became a believer. Pieces went for good prices to a number of people including a sculpture and an oil painting to singer Bob Dylan. Veronica arranged for me to go into the Magnolia Gallery in Oakland, California, and do a series of etchings plus an eighteen-color limited edition lithograph titled "Jazz," which is reproduced on the cover of this book.

Doing sculpture and painting was actually therapy for me. In the band business, we might work for six months straight and then lay off for three or four weeks. Painting pictures and sculpting takes up the slack for me. And of course, it is a labor of love—it's great fun. I never saw it as a commercial venture. I never expected to sell a piece of art, what with no training and no real understanding of the art world. But Veronica began to sell things, and I am too well-raised to refuse a few bucks.

What's Hitler Doing?

We don't travel from gig to gig in our old band bus anymore. Nowadays, we go by plane or car. Today, you'll find Nellie Belle VIII sitting idle at the back of our farm, right between the peach and the cherry tree rows—literally "out to pasture." We start the ole girl up from time to time, and voilà! She's ready to roll (the last rebuilt engine we installed is hardly broken in). But that hassle is in the past. We just let United Airlines or Budget Rent-a-Car worry about flat tires and mechanical repairs.

Starting in the early territory days, the band bus was always a big part of our lives. Lloyd Hunter's old tin lizzie was my first experience with band busses back in the early forties. Whereas Nellie Belle VIII is a big eight-cylinder diesel, Lloyd's ancient crate was a school bus that had seen better days. We called it the Blue Hornet, but don't ask me why. The fading and peeling paint job was actually red.

Every morning, the driver, Brother West, would pull up for our regular morning rest stop. It was time to fill up the gas tank, go to the rest room, buy a candy bar or some cigarettes, then go on to the next gig.

One of the older brothers would return to the bus with a newspaper, and someone would ask:

"Hey, Bythewood, you got the paper?"

"Yeah," Bythewood would answer.

"What's Hitler doing?"

"Same ole' shit."

"That's all?"

"Well, here's something."

"What's that?"

"White folks is still in the lead."

We'd all chuckle, although we'd heard the routine before. And would sure hear it again and again.

It's fifty years later, and white folks are still in the lead. No meaningful change for most Black folks.

If the late Jimmy Bythewood could see what's happening today, I'm sure he would be astonished and appalled to find Hitler stirring again in Europe. The bastard is doing a Dracula on us!

One morning, while going through the news, Bythewood said, "It says here, that bunch of peckerwoods beat some poor nigger half to death for stealing a bridle down in Alabama."

"Dirty motherfuckers!" growled Preston Love.

"Hey Bonesky," Harrington Ham called out, "You know all about religious stuff, so how do you think God feels about the way we're treated?"

Bonesky shot Ham a look of disgust.

"God's got too much other shit to worry about," saxophonist Ole Pardner chirped in.

Many years ago, a group of theologians asked British biologist J. B. S. Haldane a similar question. Haldane reportedly responded with "God has an inordinate fondness for beetles." When we consider the fact that there are many, many more beetles in the world than any other animal form, untold zillions of 'em, and more new varieties being identified constantly, then maybe God does have too much other shit to worry about. This thought alone is enough to knock some of the self-centered arrogance out of us, but I'm sure it won't.

Beetles outnumber humans many times over, but humans are proliferating at a very dangerous pace. The earth's population of people will double within the next forty years. And while on the subject of terrestrial life forms other than homo sapiens, I am reminded of how many species of insects, birds, mammals, fish, and plants are forever being pushed out of existence for the sake of profit. The most severe and wholesale destruction is probably occurring in the world's rain forests, but human expansion and pollution is mowing down valuable life forms everywhere. More people are aware of the plants and animals that are threatened with extinction and the tragedy of countless species already lost than at any time in the past. But there have always been a few individuals trying to sound the alarm. In 1863, scientist Alfred Russell Wallace wrote, "If we don't preserve the numerous forms of life on the planet, future ages will certainly look back on us as a people so immersed in the pursuit of wealth as to be blind to higher considerations."

Organic Apple Juice label. Out of concern for the environment, Otis has turned to organic farming. He and his son Nick produce "Johnny Otis Organic Apple Juice," distributed by Nocturne Farm in Sebastopol, California, 95472, and available at The Johnny Otis Market/Deli in Sebastopol.

One final word about the worldwide population explosion. I am not competent to discuss the dire threat of human overpopulation with any scientific authority. (And I'm a fine one to talk, what with all the kids I helped to bring into the world). But I've got enough sense to see that if we don't soon drastically control the pervasive sprawl and spread of the human race, we won't have to concern ourselves with wars, racism, homelessness, religious hatred, drugs, crime, hurricanes, earthquakes, ethnic strife, the economy, the budget deficit, the savings and loan criminals, totalitarian communism, predatory capitalism, or fascism. Because we won't be here.

PART 6

THE LOS ANGELES
REBELLION AND THE
POLITICS OF RACE

By Any Means

If George Washington had coined the term, "By Any Means Necessary," it would be recorded in American history books as indelibly as Lincoln's Gettysburg Address. It is okay for whites to declare that they would do anything to be free of oppression, but Blacks do not have that same option. Blacks are permitted to wring their hands and bemoan their fate, but don't start talking about doing something drastic to get the man's foot off your neck. Whites can exalt about "bombs bursting in air," but if a Black man or woman so much as suggests kickin' some ass to get free, the right wing bristles, and the liberals are pained.

During the sixties in Los Angeles, when Malcolm X used to call our small group of activists together at Richard Morris's house, he would say, "If you've got a chain around your neck and your wife and children are shackled, and your mother and father and your people are chained, and you've tried all the acceptable methods of getting free and nothing works, then you either stay chained forever or you look at the alternative—breaking free by any means necessary."

After a short pause, he would mischievously add, "Now, I know that some of you brothers are not ready for such a thought, but. . . ." We would all react, "Yes, we are . . . yes, we are!" Then with a twinkle in his eye he would state, "Well, let's just say that those of us in this room are prepared to accept 'by any means necessary' as a valid tool for our freedom, but the preachers and the teachers and the creatures among us have scared our people into submission. Someday, though, and it won't be long, we will wake up. Someday, when all else has failed, we will break our chains and gain our manhood by any means necessary."

After twenty-five years of dormancy, the spirit of Malcolm X is stirring among young African Americans. Malcolm X T-shirts are popular. Malcolm's philosophy is rapped out by young recording artists. The

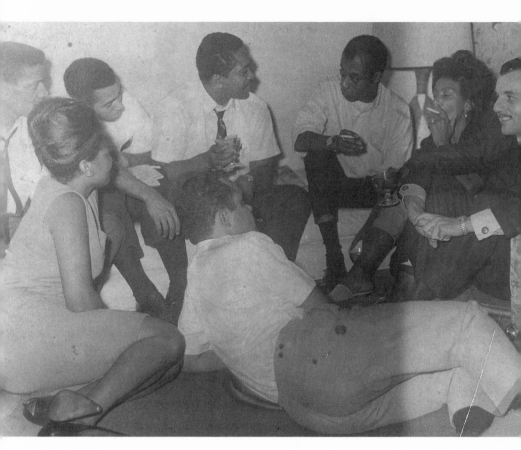

In discussion group with James Baldwin, the early 1960s.

young in the streets don't talk much about Martin Luther King if they talk about him at all. The gang members consider "turn the other cheek" a failed policy. During the L.A. uprising, a young gang homey told a TV reporter, "I don't wanna hear none of that 'We Shall Overcome' shit!"

Out of the violence and the tragedy of the Rodney King event has emerged an unlikely development. Members of the rival Crips and Bloods gangs have decided they should come together and stop killing one another. Should this truce hold and develop into a firm partnership, the Los Angeles Police Department may be looking at their worst nightmare come true.

T-shirts, slogans, and rap records promoting Malcolm X's philosophy will amount to very little as long as African Americans are waging war against one another. Malcolm's exhortations to stand up, clean up, shun drugs, honor our women, and stick together can have little meaning in a community racked by gang and drug warfare.

Recently, in Los Angeles, I heard an elderly Black man say to a group of very young gang members, "Some little brother down the street who wears a different color bandana ain't your enemy." As he was talking, an L.A.P.D. squad car with two white cops cruised slowly by. The old man nodded at the police car. "Think about it," he said.

We Sing Too Much

I didn't go sit at any southern white racist lunch counters in the 60s, and if it happens again, I ain't goin' this time either. Not because I'm such a coward. I am a scary motherfucker, it's true, but I would take a beating and probably risk dying too, if I thought it would free my people. I say "probably," because I don't think any of us knows how we would react in case of a "tie," like "All right, you great martyr, stick your head in this furnace while I slam the door and your people are free!" Sh-i-i-i-et! I hope I never have to find out.

When I say my people, I'm not referring to the few black million-aires among us; I mean the PEOPLE. Those God-forsaken hundreds of thousands upon hundreds of thousands who live in poverty with no help and no hope.

Malcolm X, Ron Karenga, Stokely Carmichael, H. Rap Brown, Bobby Seale, and a handful of others warned us that passive resis-tance and "turn the other cheek" were false premises. They foretold that Whitey would pass a law or two, hand out a few crumbs and then it would be business as usual. And that is exactly what has happened.

Oh, but wait a minute. Didn't it feel good to join hands and sing "we shall overcome!" It gave us a chance to sing, which we dearly love to do, and to throw in those soulful gospelish embellishments. You know, those little twirls and turns that Black folk do instinctively, just like fall-ing off a log—and white folks can't get to save their lives—although they keep trying, God help us!

Malcolm cracked us up in a speech at Los Angeles's 2nd Baptist Church when he said "We sing too much anyhow!" We laughed at the quip, because we knew that as long as we're singing and inspiring one another with beautiful black melodies we don't leave ourselves much time to get out and be part of the struggle.

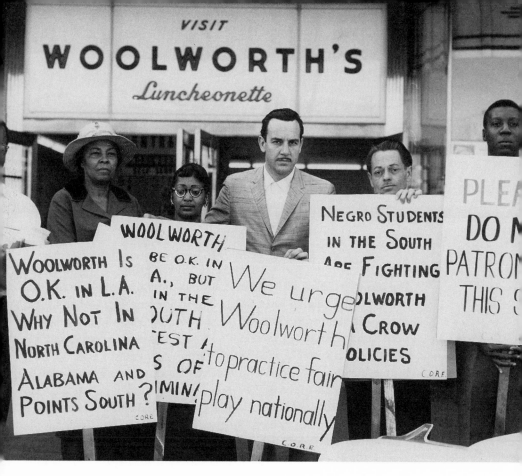

Picketing in support of lunch counter sit-ins, the early 1960s.

I am a staunch Alice Walker fan. Her short story "The Hell with Dying" is as poignant and powerful as anything I've ever read. I'm not that thrilled, however, with *The Color Purple*—especially the movie version with the stereotypical Hollywood finale where all the spiritually up-lifted "darkies" leave the juke joint and march to church, just a-singin' away. There we go singing again. Only this time, it's an insulting bit of Hollywood bullshit which wouldn't, couldn't, and shouldn't happen in a million years.

L. A. Cops:
To Protect and Serve

Los Angeles Police Chief Daryl Gates would have us believe that the Rodney King beating was a rare and isolated event. In a way he's right. It was very out of the ordinary. It was uniquely special because somebody videotaped the incident. Other than the miracle of someone being on hand with a camera, the vicious beating of a citizen by L.A. cops was business as usual. Anyone who lives in the poorest sections of the city knows that many of the police who patrol their areas function as predators on the prowl. This has nothing to do with containing lawlessness or keeping the peace. It is an evil game. A skin game. You don't have to be involved in criminal activity to become a punching bag. Just be there and be Black. Everyone knows there are criminal enterprises operating in parts of the ghetto. The fact that we have ghettos explains why we have crime. The ghettos also contain uncared-for sick, crushing poverty, crumbling schools, undernourished children, and abject hopelessness.

Any drug dealer who is busted runs the risk of going to prison. But before he ever gets to court, he runs the risk of being beaten to a pulp. For that matter, so does any law-abiding Black citizen.

Even one or two maladjusted racists running loose within the police department would be intolerable, but there are more than one or two L.A.P.D. Hitlers wearing the blue uniform and carrying a gun and a club. Young Black men are their special prey. Latino men are targeted too, of course, but not with the same malice. I should point out, however, that there is a measure of equal opportunity at work here. L.A. cops will occasionally beat the holy shit out of white and Asian men also.

Many L.A. cops seem to feel that their gun and badge give them license to apprehend AND mete out punishment. They are judge and jury squads. Never mind that some of the men they nab are innocent of any wrongdoing—UPSIDE YOUR HEAD, anyhow! To point out that their job is to apprehend suspects and the judging and punishing should be left to others, would be confusing the issue with facts, given the average cop mentality. Dirty Harry lives. To play judge, jury, and executioner is illegal activity, but the loose canons in the L.A.P.D. have been doing it for fifty years that I know of.

In the aftermath of the Rodney King beating, the general public has gotten a glimpse of how racist L.A. cops actually are. The police head-quarters' recorded messages with references to "Gorillas in the Mist" and the "I got me one" cracks are typical. Officer Stacy Koon's excuse for beating Rodney King so unmercifully is that King shook his buttocks at a white female officer in a sexually suggestive way. This, Koon said, caused the woman to fear a "Mandingo" danger. No, this isn't 1921 Mississippi when valorous white men protected white womanhood against "Black bucks." This is 1992 Los Angeles—but not much has changed.

The whole world saw the tape of the Rodney King beating. There was widespread shock and outrage both in America and overseas. Months went by. The trial venue was shifted from L.A. to suburban Simi Valley. By now, whites are very uncomfortable with seeing the tape over and over again. A jury without even one Black member acquitted the four accused officers of the charges. The racist verdict ignites the deadliest urban uprising in recent history.

Suddenly whites here and there are muttering that we didn't see the entire tape. Putting a new spin on the happenings will help assuage their guilt feelings and the frustration they feel when seeing the tape. In the earlier part of the tape that was never aired, they say, Rodney King can be seen lunging at the cops. We, the public, saw only part of the tape. The jurors saw the whole tape. That's why the verdict was acquittal. Here we go again, white folks getting themselves off the hook. In other words, don't believe your eyes, believe this bullshit about Rodney King lunging at the cops.

Big, bad, unarmed Rodney King lunged at those four poor little white boys who had only guns, clubs, and fifteen other cops standing by to back them up.

What would have happened if Rodney King had been white and the four cops who bashed him senseless had been Black?

If I'm not mistaken, the motto of the L.A.P.D. is "To Protect and Serve." With that in mind, let's think about what L.A. Police Sergeant Stacy Koon has to say in his new book. You remember him, don't you? He's one of the white thugs who pummeled Rodney King on the video.

"I am not a racist," he says, "and I do not condone or tolerate racism." He also claims in an interview, "In society there's the sexual prowess

Johnny Otis and vocalist Barbara Morrison, 1975.

of Blacks on the old plantations of the South and intercourse between Blacks and whites on the plantation. And that's where the fear comes in, because he's Black."

Elsewhere, this protector and server of the people of Los Angeles, who declares he's not a racist, describes what he saw Rodney King do. "He grabbed his butt with both hands and began to shake and gyrate his fanny in a sexually suggestive fashion." In the next sentence, he reads California Highway Patrol Officer Melanie Singer's mind. "As King sexually gyrated," he states, "A mixture of fear and offense overcame Melanie. The fear was of a Mandingo sexual encounter."

There is a fear here, all right, the age-old white man's fear that a Black man might get to his woman and the even larger fear that she might like it. By putting words in the woman officer's mouth, Koon puts his mind at ease. If he can believe that the white woman took offense and was frightened, he is no longer threatened by the Black man's sexuality.

I neither know nor care if Rodney King sexually gyrated but sexually gyrating while you're getting your brains beat out sounds like just one more lie.

For white people who believe that African Americans threaten their comfortable existence and are a menace to society, I could write ten books and it wouldn't affect their mentality one bit. This book then, is aimed at the white people who want to be on the right side of this dilemma. If this book were targeted toward Black people, I could save my energy, they already know this stuff—if not specifically then instinctively and by experience. I am not presumptuous or arrogant about presenting my opinions. I have lived for over sixty years in the heart of the African American community, most of that time in the Los Angeles ghetto area. My wife, my children, and my grandchildren are Black. I know what I'm talking about, and, furthermore, I know I'm right.

The Watts riot was a sensation for a short time. Then the excitement and the memory faded. Now, thirty years and two riots later, I wonder if events have shaped a sizeable section of our white population into wanting to deal with the truth? I hope so, because the truth is that racism is devastating our African American population and in the process, cutting the heart out of American democracy. This is the ugly truth. There are no two sides to this question.

This whole mess is not a recent phenomenon. Black Americans have been oppressed and dispossessed, both during and after slavery, for 400 years. The various devices for holding African Americans down are always with us. They may change form from time to time, but the effect is constant.

Malcolm X said, "Racism is like a Cadillac. The 1960 Cadillac doesn't look like the 1921 Cadillac, but it is still a Cadillac; it has simply changed form." This applies to the 1993 Cadillac, also, I might add.

In 1965, a white friend suggested I title my first book, *Listen, Whitey*. An even angrier person offered, *Listen, Honkey!* I settled on *Listen to the Lambs*. This time the title is *Upside Your Head!* Things have changed. The ante is up. We've got a generation of street gangsters who aren't afraid to die. If it comes to it, they will learn the art of guerilla warfare. I'm sure a major nightmare for the L.A.P.D. is the idea of the competing gangs—the Crips and the Bloods—forming an alliance.

An all-out uprising would suck everyone into the conflict. Ultimately, it would involve more than the homies in the hood and the cops. I'm hoping it never comes to this, but as long as the misery in the ghetto deepens, the possibility of a blood bath is real. But don't just take my word for it. Listen to the more militant and thoughtful young male and female rappers. They may chill your blood a bit, but sometimes a candid and icy tonic is good for the blood—and the soul.

Black Conservatives

When I look at the recent political phenomenon of people who count themselves "Black conservatives," I am fascinated and dismayed. I don't mean simply Black Republicans. We've long had African Americans in the GOP—conservatives in the traditional sense. This is a natural outcome of the two-party system. I'm talking about the Black individuals, some of them highly placed, who cleave to the coat tails of the powerful white fascists in the extreme right wing of the Republican Party.

What could possibly motivate any Black woman or man to move in that unlikely direction? Do they believe that concentrating the bulk of the country's wealth in the hands of a tiny elite is a good thing? Maybe they're convinced that kissing Mister Charlie's ass will cause some of the big bucks to rub off on them, and damn the consequences to the American Dream and democracy. Are they convinced that turning back the clock on civil rights and chipping away at the Bill of Rights is in the best interests of their people or the country at large? How can they go along with cold-blooded slashing of social services to impoverished Blacks and other disadvantaged Americans?

Perhaps dismay is not the best word to describe how I feel when I contemplate this new breed of Black conservatives. Nausea comes to mind. But they certainly are fascinating. How can one not be fascinated by such a personality. I mean, a Black Reaganite—that's quite a contradiction in terms.

There's nothing particularly fascinating about most European Americans. They are usually, to one degree or another, racist, ethnocentric, and seemingly unable (certainly unwilling) to embrace the concept of brotherhood in real life. They are big on lip service to lofty ideas about equality. Every Sunday they fill their houses of worship and piously agree with sermons about love and brotherhood, but living the prin-

Johnny Otis makes a contribution to Daisy Bates of the National Association for the Advancement of Colored People to help the school desegregation fight in Little Rock, Arkansas.

ciples is another matter. At the same time, they are, of course, over all decent folk. That is, most of them are law-abiding, honest citizens. They care for their loved ones, pay their bills, and so on. But woven right into their basic decency is an indecent attitude toward African Americans and other non-whites, although they don't seem to realize it. They have artfully managed to convince themselves that they are decent and nonracist in this respect. Blaming the victim for his plight is an old story in America. Once they swallow the lies about Blacks being more violent, prone to criminal activity, lazy, less intelligent, unqualified, inferior culturally, a threat to their jobs, and so forth, they are able to purge themselves of any conscious guilt.

When we travel to Europe I notice a lot of holier than thou attitudes concerning racism in the United States. The only reason open racism isn't as evident in Europe is that there are no significant numbers of Black people living there. Give them a large population of non-whites, and I'm sure Europeans would be as anti-Black as European-Americans. They're all Europeans, after all. A hyphen is all that separates them. One must understand that it's not just Skinheads and Neo-Nazis who are giving non-Europeans hell on the continent nowadays. There is that less visible mass of people who quietly discriminate against North Africans and Arabs in France, the West Indians in England, and the Asians, Turks, and Africans in Germany. Now they have become more open. Jean-Marie Le Pen's racist National Front received almost 14 percent of the vote in the March 1992 elections. Racists in Germany have launched deadly assaults on "foreigners." In the United States, Nazi/Ku Klux Klanner David Duke polled more than 50 percent of the white vote in a Louisiana gubernatorial election. His anti-Black messages, some veiled, some not so veiled, have great appeal to Euro-Americans.

Quayle

Like many other people who are concerned about seeing the American Dream finally realized, I continue to try to do what I can through my radio show, on interviews, and in day-to-day conversations. But I am less convinced of the outcome today than I was years ago. The rich-get-richer and the poor-get-poorer trend in the United States is the poisonous main ingredient in America's terminal sickness of the soul.

During his Murphy Brown tirade, Vice-President Quayle said, "It would be absolutely wrong to blame it (the L.A. riot) on the growth and success most Americans enjoyed during the 1980s." The Los Angeles uprising and the deep social unrest among America's poor is caused, he claimed, by "the poverty of values" in the country. By claiming that most Americans enjoyed growth and success in the eighties, he reveals himself as a bald-faced liar or an ignorant airhead. Most Americans did not enjoy growth and success in the eighties. The richest one percent of the country raked in sixty percent of the wealth. An additional fourteen percent of the money wound up in the pockets of the richest two percent, and another twenty percent of the goodies went to the wealthiest twenty percent.

In spite of my lowly beginnings as a depression child in a poor family, leaving school in the 9th grade, and scuffling like hell to pay the rent and feed my family most of my adult life, I seem to know many things that the vice-president of the most technologically advanced nation in the world does not know. (The president too, for that matter.) That's interesting, because as a college graduate, a silver-spoon-in-the-mouth member of a super wealthy family, and a highly placed government official, Quayle should have access to the truth in these matters. Unless, of course, he chooses to ignore and distort the facts.

Trying to talk to the average American about these things is a trying task. Most of us have been conditioned from the cradle, and at times, we act as our own worst enemy. We say, "I read it in the paper," as though quoting holy, sacred scripture. And surely many, many people conclude, the president or vice- president of America are to be believed above some jive-ass, Johnny Otis or any other noncredible musician, artist, street person, butcher, baker, or candlestick maker. Most of the prevailing wisdom is that our highly placed officials are brilliant, able, and knowledgeable, or they wouldn't be highly placed. They don't know or care that most elections are bought and paid for by the rich and operate on an insinuating, subliminal level using mini-second radio and television sight and sound bytes. The members of the privileged class who buy the elections could care less if their candidate is an intellectual cripple as long as he (they are almost always men) does his ideological duty in an obedient manner.

If Pablo Casals, Lester Young, Barbara Streisand, Vladimir Horo-witz, Duke Ellington, Louis Armstrong, Ella Fitzgerald, Wynton Mar-salis, or Luciano Pavoratti had a social or political point to make, it would not be taken seriously. Even if they espoused the view that water is wet, the idea would be taken with a grain of salt. After all, they're just musicians, what the hell do they know? Jessie Jackson enjoys a strong position in the minds of a large group of Americans, but even he is viewed by many as some kind of "Negro" preacher with a personal axe to grind.

In the unlikely event that Quayle is not a liar and is, in fact, simply stupid and misinformed, I should like to point out that one-parent fami-lies are not the reason we have violent rebellion and rage in the inner cities. PLAIN OLD POVERTY, not poverty of values is the reason for social decay, urban unrest, hopelessness, rage, violence, and rebellion. All these negative things and more grow out of economic injustice and racism. Crushing poverty is the cancer that is eating at America's soul. Our problems are not caused by the welfare system or Lyndon Johnson's Great Society programs. Never mind White House Spokesman Marvin Fitzwater's inane sputterings to the contrary.

Crappy schools, inadequate and nonexistent social programs, mil-lions of people without decent medical care (many with NO medical care), unpunished rich criminals, unemployment, inflation—these are the things that unrest and riots are made of. Not women (and some men too) gamely struggling to raise their kids without a mate. The Murphy Browns of the world should be admired and, when necessary, assisted.

And while we're on the subject, one would think that Quayle, Bush, and that entire crew of preppy, right-to-life rich kids would endorse Murphy Brown's action. After all, she didn't have an abortion, did she? Nor did she grant eleventh-hour pardons to members of her inner circle who were suspected of criminal activity.

Maya's Poem

Seeing my good friend Maya Angelou reciting her poem of hope at the Clinton inauguration, I thought, hey! Just when we were shuddering at the thought of four more years in the bottomless pit of Bush/Quayle, here comes a young governor out of Arkansas who invites a powerful Black female presence to compose a theme for his upcoming presidency. I haven't seen Maya since she spoke at one of our Landmark Church dinners in the early 1980s, but when I do, I'm gonna say "Hey baby, back in the 1960s when Phyllis and I would take our kids and you would bring your little boy and we would all go down to the beach, could we ever imagine what the future would bring?"

That an American president would commission and endorse a poem that contained these words is quite a change:

> Each new hour holds new chances
> For new beginnings
> Do not be wedded forever
> To fear, yoked eternally
> To brutishness.
> The horizon leans forward,
> Offering you space to place new steps of
> change.

I'm told that Clinton thinks Kenny G is a great saxophone talent. Oh well, he's still young, and maybe he just hasn't heard Lester Young, Ben Webster, Charlie Parker, Zoot Sims, or Sonny Rollins yet.

Which reminds me, during the 1988 Republican convention in New Orleans, we were in the middle of a three-month engagement at the Fairmont Hotel. One night, a fellow came in and told me that Vice-President Bush would like to have my band play for a big celebration party. I thought to myself, "Who does this motherfucker think he's bullshittin'? George Bush has never heard of Johnny Otis!"

I said, "Yes, of course." But he meant play free. And I don't play free for Republicans—or Democrats. The next day I got a call on the phone from a man who introduced himself as Lee Atwater. At the time the name didn't register. The architect of the Willie Horton poison hadn't become famous yet. He wanted us free also, so I told him to go screw too. Many of the New Orleans artists did the gig, for free. I hated to see that.

I'll make a deal with the Democrats right now. If this administration lives up to its promise, I'll play the 1997 inauguration free. Wait a minute, they've probably never heard of me either!

American Fascism

One of my relatives on the white side of our family thinks there is a lot of good will toward black people among American whites. I don't believe that. There is some good will from whites, of course, but it is rare and it is usually conditional. She probably believes this because she and her circle of upper middle-class friends are full of good will and caring. They probably discuss the racial question and arrive at decent conclusions. Some of her circle are probably African American and other minorities. These are good people with good instincts, but to my way of thinking this is not so much good will as it is lip service. If there is so much good will toward blacks on the part of whites, why is it that after four hundred years the plight of most African Americans is still desperate and getting worse?

In addition to being depressed about the social situation in America, I have just about given up hope of things ever really improving. We are so far down the line toward being the North American version of South Africa and Nazi Germany, that my mind tells me it's too late for justice and equality. In spite of all the evidence to the contrary however, my heart won't give up the hope that somehow, someday, events will lead to brotherhood. But I'm not holding my breath.

The general populations of early South Africa and Germany were not aware that apartheid and Nazism were evil systems. They saw something in it for themselves. The suppression of blacks in South Africa and Jews in Germany fed the racist sickness in those societies and promised to improve the lot of white South Africans and Aryan Germans. Before long, apartheid and Nazi fascism became a comfortable way of life. South African whites took all the valuable land and forced black people into barren "homelands." If this tweaked the conscience of a few whites, there was always biblical justification to fall back on. The Christian churches of South Africa very conveniently trotted out scriptures to show that God had given dominion to superior whites over inferior blacks, and if God said it, it was okay.

In Germany the new world order (that term has a current and chilling familiarity) declared that Jews had all this property and money they had gained by dealing dishonestly with Aryans, and anyhow, they had killed Christ, so, it was all right to kill them. Here comes God to the rescue of racists again!

In America today, it is not fashionable to blurt out racist slurs. Two racist presidents in a row have put a new spin on the business of prejudice. While anti-blackness is the order of the day, nobody stands on a corner, as was done in earlier times, and shouts "Get them niggers!" Americans now express themselves with code words and euphemisms. The majority of white people quietly believe, to one degree or another, that African Americans are welfare queens, Willie Horton rapists, lazy, prone to be criminals, morally and intellectually inferior. With these attitudes, it is no big deal to tacitly ignore, abandon and dispossess black people.

Final Statement

Sometimes I wonder, what the hell good is it if nothing has changed in over fifty years. I mean, nothing of any real consequence where black people are concerned.

At this stage of my life, I should be cruising on out as comfortably as possible, but it's not that simple because the same old hypocritical, All-American white man's hypocrisy is still stuck in my throat and I can't spit it out.

Could I have even dreamed back in the forties that half a century later my people would still be trapped and oppressed?

Recently, we received an invitation to a Fourth of July Bar—B-Q. If the people who were hosting the party were not such nice folks, and if I were just a little more uncouth, I'd tell them where they could shove their Fourth of July celebration. Independence, whose independence?

I'm about as thrilled with the Fourth of July concept as I am about Columbus Day. I find nothing to celebrate in the fact that chicken-shit Christopher Columbus and his motley crew opened up the new world to the Europeans so they could ravage the environment, destroy Native American culture, and enslave millions of Africans.

As I was reading aloud from the Fourth of July invitation, my son Nicky and my friend George Trueheart Unsworth exclaimed, "Sheeeit!" in unison. An American Indian and a Black man with the same instant reaction. I feel, it is important to stop sanitizing our statements and start giving vent to our true feelings. When whites begin to understand how most black folks feel, they might want to give this whole system another thought. Sister Souljah speaks for a great many of us when she says "I was not born to make white people comfortable." The angriest soul rappers are promising to meet the man in the streets. Whatever this portends for the future, it shows very vividly that a new breed of young black men and women are tired of taking this shit and are ready to defend themselves to the death.

If any of my former church members are scandalized by some of their ex-pastor's rough language in this book, so be it. And if my white friends resent the ideas expressed here, so be it. It is time that whites realized what it's going to cost them to keep African Americans in the second-class citizen category. Jesus didn't say we should forgive unrepentant motherfuckers who have their heels on our children's necks. And if you think I'm angry, living a comfortable middle-class existence, just think how the millions trapped in poverty feel.

I'd like a little peace of mind, but no. . . .

Johnny Otis sculpting (Stephan Rockwerk, by permission).

Index

UNIVERSITY PRESS OF NEW ENGLAND publishes books under its own imprint and is the publisher for Brandeis University Press, Brown University Press, University of Connecticut, Dartmouth College, Middlebury College Press, University of New Hampshire, University of Rhode Island, Tufts University, University of Vermont, and Wesleyan University Press.

George Lipsitz is Professor of Ethnic Studies at the University of California, San Diego. He is the author of *A Life in the Struggle: Ivory Perry and the Culture of Opposition*, winner of the Anisfield-Wolf Award as the best book in race relations in 1988, as well as the Kayden Prize for the best book in the humanities published by a university press. His other books include *Time Passages: Collective Memory and American Popular Culture, Class and Culture in Cold War America*, and *The Sidewalks of St. Louis*. He serves with Susan McClary and Robert Walser as editors of the Music Culture series.

Library of Congress Cataloging-in-Publication Data

Otis, Johnny, 1921–
   Upside your head! : rhythm and blues on Central Avenue / by Johnny Otis.
   p.   cm.—(Music culture)
   Includes index.
   ISBN 0–8195–5263–1
   1. Otis, Johnny, 1921– . 2. Blues musicians—United States—
Biography. I. Title. II. Series.
ML419.O85A3   1993
781.643′092—dc20
  ∞   93–13611